Laurence Oliphant

Masollam - A Problem of the Period

A Novel. Vol. III

Laurence Oliphant

Masollam - A Problem of the Period
A Novel. Vol. III

ISBN/EAN: 9783744661669

Printed in Europe, USA, Canada, Australia, Japan

Cover: Foto ©Thomas Meinert / pixelio.de

More available books at **www.hansebooks.com**

M A S O L L A M;

A PROBLEM OF THE PERIOD.

A NOVEL

BY

LAURENCE OLIPHANT

AUTHOR OF 'PICCADILLY,' 'ALTIORA PETO,' ETC. ETC.

IN THREE VOLUMES

VOL. III.

WILLIAM BLACKWOOD AND SONS
EDINBURGH AND LONDON
MDCCCLXXXVI

CONTENTS OF THE THIRD VOLUME.

PART II.—*continued.*

CHAP.   PAGE

IV. AMINA ENTERS UPON HER MISSION, . . 1

V. SANTALBA DISCOURSES ON THE "PROBLEM
OF THE PERIOD" WITH THE SHEIKH, . 24

VI. SHEIKH SHIBLEY MAKES A PROPOSAL OF
MARRIAGE, ... 40

VII. WHEN GREEK MEETS GREEK, . . . 63

VIII. CONSPIRACY AND TREACHERY, . . . 83

IX. A DOMESTIC CRISIS, ... 104

X. THE TRAGEDY, ... 126

XI. SHEIKH SHIBLEY FAILS IN HIS PLOT, . . 146

XII. THE KHATEEB COMES TO SHEIKH SHIBLEY'S
AID, ... 166

XIII. AMINA ASSERTS THE RIGHTS OF WOMAN, . 184

XIV. A PARTY OF RESCUE FROM THE WEST
ARRIVES AT TERAYA, ... 204

XV. THE GRAND COUNCIL, ... 224

XVI. CONCLUSION, ... 245

PART II.

(Continued.)

PART IV.

MASOLLAM:

A PROBLEM OF THE PERIOD.

CHAPTER IV.

AMINA ENTERS UPON HER MISSION.

At this moment a low tapping was heard in an outer apartment as of some one desiring to attract attention, and afraid of intruding. Santalba hastily disengaged himself from the sheikh's embrace, saying as he did so, "It is Amina."

"You called me," she said, as he met her.

"Yes, my child, I desired your presence. I have that to say to your uncle which it is important that you should hear. Much as I should wish it, I cannot linger long here, and

we three have many things to communicate
to each other which are best said in these silent hours.   The sheikh has already told me
enough to fill my heart with joy, for I feel
that I am leaving you with one who will be
more to you than any earthly father; while,
with the knowledge and training you have
received, you can be not my daughter only,
but the guide and support of his old age.
Meantime I want him to know and understand
you before I leave you together."

So saying he led her to the divan on which
her uncle was seated, and placed her by his side.
The old man received her kindly, but cast a
glance of surprise and inquiry on his friend.

"I have deemed the presence of your niece
necessary at this stage of our conversation,"
he said in reply to it; "in the first place,
because her experiences, which it is fitting that
you should now hear, have been not less remarkable than yours or mine; and in the second,
because, for reasons which I will presently
explain, with her at my side, I shall be able
to enter upon the considerations suggested by
your narrative, aided by a faculty of perception of which I should be deprived by her

absence. I will leave her to tell you her own story, merely saying, by way of preface to it, that on that eventful night when the attack took place upon this village, and I believed that you, as well as her father and mother, had fallen a victim to the fury of the assailants, I was happily the means of snatching this child from the grasp of one of them, at the moment when his knife was at her throat, and I fled with her to Damascus. Seeking earnestly the divine guidance in regard to the disposition which I should make of her, I perceived that she had been intrusted to me as a sacred charge; and in this Daoud Effendi Masollam, with whom, as you know, I always lodged when in that city, entirely agreed with me. So strongly did he feel on the subject, that he proposed to adopt her as his own daughter, and to train her in the knowledge of those truths which were even then unfolding their vast possibilities to our enthusiasm. Having, I believe, then, with reason, the most complete confidence in his purity and singleness of motive, and the highest admiration for his wonderful gifts, I thankfully accepted the offer, on the understanding, however, that

should the occasion present itself when I
could take charge of her education in Europe
she should be sent to me, as I desired she
might supplement her oriental studies with
the advantages of training under the influences of Western civilisation. On my return
to France I married, and all the more important years of her life she passed under the
immediate care and supervision of myself and
of that saintly woman whom God bestowed
upon me as a most precious gift; who was,
and still remains, the light and inspiration of
my life, and whose mantle has now fallen upon
Amina. On the death of my wife, I restored
our charge to the care of the Masollams, who
were in Paris at the time, and she returned
with them to Damascus. Her history from
that time to the present she will tell you
herself. I must add, however, that it had
been arranged between Masollam and myself
that her origin and race should not be revealed to her, but that she should be taught
to regard herself as one whose duties were
not to any special country or people, but to
the world at large, to which sentiment she
should be trained to subordinate even her

natural affections towards those whom she considered her parents."

"My difficulty was," interrupted Amina, with an affectionate glance at Santalba, "to avoid loving those who lived in Paris, and whom I knew were not my real parents, more than those who lived in Damascus, and whose child I believed myself to be. Still my devotion to, admiration for, and faith in Daoud Effendi were unbounded; and if I did not entertain the same sentiments for my supposed mother, she commanded my entire respect, not unmingled with a certain awe, and I believed that the reserve she ever manifested towards me proceeded from a fear lest her natural maternal affection should interfere with that higher love which she professed for the cause to which she had dedicated her life."

Amina then proceeded to describe her early experiences and training as bearing upon the service to which she had willingly determined to devote herself, as soon as her faculties had so far developed as to enable her to comprehend its scope and methods, and explained how the habit of blind and unquestioning obedience to those whom she gradually came

to regard as morally infallible, at last reached
such a point as to deprive her of all faculty of
private judgment. Latterly, she said, this
assumption of impeccability on the part of
the Masollams had arrived at such a pitch,
that she felt that any mental criticism of their
acts on her part amounted to absolute dis-
loyalty to them and the cause they represented ; and she therefore steadily refused to
attend to any objections which her own moral
sense suggested in regard to their conduct.
She the more readily slid into this attitude
of mind because the moral change—the operation of which she fancied she observed in her
parents, and which was not without its de-
teriorating effect on her own conscience—was
so gradual and subtle as to be difficult of de-
tection. At last her own moral faculty had
become so perverted, that she honestly believed
that doubts and criticisms were infernal temptations, which she now perceived to have been
the suggestions of conscience and the voice
of God speaking within her.

" Does it not strike you as strange," interposed the old sheikh, " that God should allow
those who have no desire on earth but to find

Him and do His will, to be so far deceived in
their efforts as to mistake His voice within
them for the voice of the Tempter, whom we
in our religion call the Rival, or Antagonist?"

"That is a point I have had deeply to consider," replied Santalba. "It has been suggested by my own experience, and by that of
others for whom I have the highest esteem and
the warmest affection, both in the Churches
and outside of them."

"And what is the conclusion at which you
have arrived?"

"As it is in the nature of an attempted
explanation of the methods employed by the
Deity in His dealings with His creatures, I
would speak with the utmost diffidence and
reverence," answered Santalba. "As the motives by which men are actuated are subtle
and infinitely varied and complex, it is evident that in each case the divine treatment
must be adapted to meet special conditions;
and that as new and higher truth descends
into the world, it can only do so at first in
an extremely attenuated form, otherwise it
would produce a moral shock which would
convulse humanity beyond its bearing powers;

and as it can only be conveyed through human
instruments, these are in the beginning few in
number, often obscure and unknown, who are
silently and almost unconsciously to themselves sowing the new seed on soil only here
and there prepared to receive it. In this
service they encounter innumerable obstacles,
and a fierce and persistent opposition from the
powers of darkness, who seek to intercept the
descent of the new rays of light. What they
do, in fact, is to temper them to the bearing
point. This consideration is the one great consolation of those who seek to make themselves,
as it were, burning-glasses for the concentra-
tion of that light. They are wearied and worn
out, and are apt to be disappointed and chilled
by the gloom and the coldness which seems to
neutralise all their efforts; and they wonder
why, if they do indeed possess God's truth,
it makes such slow progress, and warms so
few hearts. But it warms some; and each
new one is a fresh spark added to that divine
fire which, if it is consuming, is also vivifying
and comforting, but which, if it spread too
rapidly, would become an overwhelming con-
flagration. It is evident that each one who

desires absolutely to be an instrument for the dissemination of an element at once so precious, and in a sense so dangerous, must be specially chosen according to his moral conditions, and can only be intrusted with so much of it as he can bear, and which he has vital energy and potency to distribute. His strength lies in his faith; for there is a faith which is a sign of strength, as there is a faith which is a sign of weakness. The faith which gives strength is that which demands nothing either from God or man. It demands no heaven; it demands no happiness—not even peace, though it gives it; it demands no success—not even visible results or rewards either here or hereafter. It commands. It commands service; unflinching, unwavering, persistent, blind service—service of God and for man. It believes in service. In incessant, uncompromising labour for human necessities—for the poorest, meanest, most practical necessities; those which shall provide all men with food and clothing,—which shall raise men and women on earth to the level of equality that they possess in the sight of God, not of each other—which shall meet the most pressing questions of the hour—political, economical, and domestic. It believes in a solution to the sociological problem; and it works for it hopefully, bravely, and persistently. That is the faith which gives strength. And because that strength manifests itself in phenomena that are strictly according to the law which accompanies a faith of this description, but which science cannot grapple with—because no scientific man can investigate the operation of the law unless he is acting under the influences of the moral forces upon which it is conditioned—it is called mystical and visionary. For the faith which is really mystical and visionary, we must turn to the faith that produces weakness. This demands everything both from God and man. It demands from God a heaven. Ay, it goes further; it demands from Him a hell, and therefore it demands also a Saviour. It demands from man a Church, where it may find comfort and priestly advice and protection, and peace and happiness arising from the fellowship and support of other believers in dogmas innumerable. This is the faith which is mystical and visionary; which crawls and supplicates for itself, and leaves the world with all

the ills that human flesh is heir to in the
position of misery it has occupied from all
time. Nevertheless there are those in these
Churches as earnestly seeking after truth as
you or I—as ready to do God's service, and
to spend and be spent for humanity as we
are. And you ask why they are left where
they are. My answer is, Because it is where
God designs that they should be. Either
because they are not yet strong enough to
exchange the old faith for the new, and need
more suffering and ordeal; or because, unknown to themselves, there is still latent some-
where in them the spiritual pride or subtle
egotism which characterises the ecclesiasticism
in which they have been reared, and to which
they are blind. They are serving God in a
certain way. For He can enlist error into His
service; and those who hold it sincerely and
conscientiously differ in His sight in no way
from us, who think we hold truth—or, at all
events, the small modicum of truth that we
can bear. It is but a question of degree with
us all. Some can hold more truth, some less.
But God does not esteem His human vessels
according to their size, or strength, or the purity

of what they hold. They are all part of Him,
made and fashioned by Him, and destined
sooner or later to feel the full joy of a union
with Him. But it is not for us to speculate
upon the methods, or the times and the sea-
sons, however near or remote, when in each
individual case this union will take place."

"Nevertheless," said Amina, "on looking
back over my past experiences, it is impossible for me sometimes not to feel harassed by
regrets. I have hitherto shrunk from paining
you by alluding to them; but after what you
have said, I hope that even mistakes, if made
with a pure motive during a period of delusion,
will not be allowed to injure the cause we
desired to serve."

"You speak to one, my child," interrupted
her uncle, "who has made greater mistakes
than you can ever have done, and who has
never ceased regretting them—the nature of
which I have already explained to our dear
friend here."

"As we are making confessions," said Santalba, "of acts done under a pressure which,
for some wise purpose, God permitted so far
to control our judgment as to pervert our

moral sense, there are probably none of us in the search after truth who have not been led astray, myself perhaps most of all. You, my dear Amina, may spare yourself the revelation you were about to make, for I know how those who, alas, have proved traitors, sought to employ you as a decoy, and to make use of your gifts and your beauty to attract those who might be fascinated by the charm of mystery which surrounded you, and so induce them to contribute their wealth to a cause advocated by a lovely woman in winning and plausible language. I know how you did violence to your own maidenly instincts in consciously using that magnetic spell with which you, in common with the purest and the basest of your sex, are endowed, to enslave those whom Masollam desired to plunder, and almost unconsciously slid into charlatanism in the effort, as you firmly believed, to win souls, with whatever means they might have at their disposal, to God's service. You caught the trick insensibly from your master. I speak feelingly, for I also contrived to do violence to my conscience at his behest. It was under his orders that I, who am by na-

ture, whatever may be my other faults, absolutely indifferent to wealth, engaged in those
commercial speculations with the elder Hartwright which were so successful to us both.
And though we were careful to adhere rigidly
to the world's standard in such matters, I was
conscious of repeatedly violating my own
higher instincts, and of justifying that vio-
lation by the reflection that I had a selfish
pride in my own high standard of honour, and
that God demanded that I should outrage it
as a sacrifice to Him.   In all this, my dear,
believe me, we have nothing to regret.   I can
guess without being told, the sufferings you
endured at the hands of the woman, who,
though enjoying the protection which her
position as his wife gave her, should never
have stood in that relation to Masollam ; and
I know how, from the moment that he accepted that relation, he began to sink, and
how both you and I, unsuspicious of the
female treachery—as, poor man, he was himself—unconsciously began to sink with him,
until at last our eyes were mercifully opened
by the recent occurrences in England.   I know
both what our mistakes and our sufferings were

during this period; but I regret nothing, for our motives were pure, and He can turn every mistaken act to good account in the future; and every spasm of agony we underwent was as it were the blast of a purifying furnace, which was needed to fit us to be the instruments we seek to be. But in order," continued Santalba, "that your uncle should understand our allusions to one whom he has been accustomed to regard as the best and purest of men, you must proceed with your story, and explain to him the circumstances under which you and your mother went separately to England, what happened to you while there, and how you came to leave it."

The sheikh listened attentively to Amina's graphic and detailed narrative, his eyes gradually expanding, and his expressive features testifying the liveliest interest and emotion, not unmixed with wonder, as she frankly described the sentiment which had grown up between herself and Clareville, and the relations which now subsisted between them.

"Mashallah!" he exclaimed, when she had concluded, "and to think you are a Druse maiden!"

"Yes, uncle; but I am the world's maiden first. I can only belong to the Druses if the Druses like to belong to me."

The old man stroked his beard thoughtfully. For a chieftain of these wild mountains he had thought and observed much, but his wildest flights of imagination had never suggested such a problem, as his newly found niece now presented to him. He cast a wistful and puzzled glance at Santalba.

"We must wait," said the latter, reading his thought; "the future contains the solution. Let us not try to work it out now. Trust her to find it. What were the words on your lips when we heard her tapping outside?"

"That the day of my deliverance, for which I had been waiting, had come."

"And even as you spoke she entered. Yes, old friend, the day, not of your deliverance alone, but of the world's deliverance has come, and it has come in the form of a woman. It could not be delivered hitherto, because the sexes were divided; but in union is strength. It is only when the sexes are united according to the divine intention that the redemptive forces for the world's deliverance can play

through them ; and it is through the operation, of the divine feminine that this union
must be achieved. This is the interpretation
of your vision of the twofold Word. Regard
women, therefore—but especially the woman
by your side—in a different light from what
you have hitherto done.

" You asked me how I could judge in regard to the character of a revelation, and
what was the test to be applied to inspiration whereby its recipient might estimate
its value. First, let him distrust it absolutely if he is not in full possession of all
his faculties. He must not produce abnormal
conditions by fasting, or unnatural diet of
any sort, calculated to damage the healthy
action of all animal functions. On the contrary, he should feel that all his senses are
exceptionally on the alert, and that his brain
is free, clear, and vigorous. Secondly, let him
reject all such inspiration as worthless, unless
the revelation it contains has a direct bearing
upon the practical solution of the world-prob-
lem. If it propounds a method of grappling
with the universal misery of to-day — if it
suggests the discovery and application of

forces hitherto unknown in nature, by which
moral and physical disease may be attacked
in their secret strongholds—let him not be
deterred by the sneer of science or the bigotry
of theologians from boldly searching out such
forces and experimenting with them. They
lie literally in the womb of nature, for they
are its procreative and its reconstructive
vigours. Thirdly, let him strive to maintain
a moral condition which may correspond as
nearly as may be to the most lofty ideal
which a conscience in hourly relation with
the Deity can suggest; and lastly, let him
associate himself devotionally and interiorly, in
absolute purity, with one of the opposite sex,
animated by like aspirations, and equally de-
sirous with himself to become receptive to the
divine afflatus, regardless of the tremendous
sacrifices which such a determination must
necessarily involve. If, with these precautions
taken, and these preliminary conditions observed, one of these co-workers, being in full
natural consciousness and intellectual vigour,
receives mental images of methods, hitherto
untried and unknown, for grappling with the
universal humanitary need, by the invocation

and application of forces in nature which have never yet been developed, and if such images are confirmed by the mental consciousness of the other co-worker, they may be safely regarded as revelations coming from a source which may be trusted; and the pair may then formulate them for their own guidance in such poor and inadequate language as our vocabularies supply, and may present them to their fellow-creatures in the form which seems best adapted to the limited scope of their apprehension.

"At this moment," continued Santalba, "the centre of the world's civilisation seethes with corruption of the foulest description, arising from the perversion of those passions which were implanted by the Deity in the human breast, for the maintenance and preservation of the race. Infernalised, the forces —of which these passions are the external manifestation—contain potencies which, if unrestrained, would destroy that race. Celestialised, they contain the only potencies which will renew it. This is the revelation we have received, and the message we have to give to the world. I say 'we,' because to each one of us here, in one form or another, it has been communicated. I appeal to the inner consciousness of both of you. To you, Amina, it was revealed through a process of experiences which have extended over years. To you, O sheikh, it declared itself in a single night in the radiance of a divine illumination. At this crisis of the world's history, the human race is brought face to face with two alternatives — union in impurity, which is infernal; or union in purity, which is divine. Yet so strangely perverted has the social moral sense become, that we who seek to prepare it for the mystery of the sacred nuptials, dare only whisper in trembling accents the cry which we should shout with joy — ' Behold, the bridegroom cometh.' The very idea of divine espousals would be considered immoral by the dwellers in the modern Babylons of this poor distraught world. Therefore, O sheikh," pursued Santalba, rising and placing Amina's hand in that of her uncle, " have I brought your niece, this virgin, whose lamp is trimmed and burning, away from the atmosphere of vice and unbelief of those cities, and have placed her as a sacred charge in your keeping. Regard her as the apple of your eye. Watch over her as one of God's vestals, to be loved and cherished and protected, ay, and even obeyed, till the hour comes when she will be summoned from her retreat to fulfil her high and holy destiny."

Sheikh Mohanna closed his eyes as Santalba ceased speaking, and remained silent for some moments, then slowly rising, he did that which no Druse man ever did before. He knelt before his niece, and bowing down his head, he took her hand and kissed it, and then pressed it reverentially on his forehead; and as he did so, Amina could no longer restrain the violence of her emotions, and she fell upon the old man's neck, and wept tears of joy and gratitude to God for this manifestation of His fatherly love and care; and suddenly a great load fell from her heart, and the cloud which had overshadowed her seemed to lift its gloomy crest and vanish into thin air. As she raised her streaming eyes to Santalba, he saw the change.

"Said I not truly, my child, when I told you but a few short hours ago that your

deliverance was at hand? No more will the
hated voice of your persecutor ring in your
ears, or the cravings of his foul passion haunt
your life. The pure and heaven-sent love of
this good old man has already surrounded you
with an atmosphere of protection so powerful
that Masollam cannot prevail against it."

"Yea, but, O friend," said Sheikh Mohanna,
rising, "she had done already more for me
than I have now done for her; for as you
placed her hand in mine, and spoke of the
divine love which had chosen her to a high
and holy destiny, and gave her so solemnly to
me in charge, and as I was mentally accept-
ing that charge, I felt that there was imparted
to me a sudden shock, like that of electricity,
which for a second caused every nerve and
fibre to tingle, but it was with delight, and
not pain; and at that moment the spirit of
darkness which had brooded over me ever
since I had allowed myself to become en-
veloped in the sphere of mysticism, and en-
slaved by its high priest, fled away; an
invisible hand seemed put forth through the
one I was holding, and struck the chains in
which I had been bound, from my hands and

feet. Suddenly I became conscious that I was a free man; and the first use I made of my freedom was to kneel before her who had achieved it."

Santalba slowly rose. "I thank Thee, my God," he said, "for having accomplished Thy work through me this night."

When, after a few moments, Sheikh Mohanna raised his head, which he also had bowed in thanksgiving, he found he was alone.

CHAPTER V.

SANTALBA DISCOURSES ON THE "PROBLEM OF
THE PERIOD" WITH THE SHEIKH.

THE sun was high in the heavens on the following day, when Santalba once more sought the chamber of his host.

"I have come," he said, "to say a few parting words, for I find that I dare not linger longer here. All over Europe, and in many parts of the east, are men who call themselves disciples of Masollam. Their principal occupation is to collect funds for the great work which it is understood that he is carrying on. It was Amina's chief duty to keep up an active correspondence with these persons, at the dictation of 'the Master'; and one of the causes of the distress she has been lately feeling, arises from the knowledge that she was called upon to make statements which she knew at the time to be false, but which, as they were dictated to her by Masollam, she did not feel entitled to question or to criticise. To remedy, so far as may be, this error, she has placed in my hands a letter addressed to them; and to as many of them as are known to me, I shall supplement it by statements of my own. The journeys which this will involve will detain me longer than I could wish from the retreat, unknown to Masollam, in which my three friends, Sebastian Hartwright, and his wife, and Clareville, are now at work. I have already parted from Amina, who has all the advice and instruction which are necessary for her guidance. She will keep me informed of what transpires here by letter, though it is probable that I shall feel without that, in a general way, how it fares with you."

"I need not say, O my brother," replied Sheikh Mohanna, "how it grieves me to part with you so soon; but I know the exacting nature of the service upon which you are engaged, and that I can best show my devotion to it by speeding you on your way. Nevertheless I have been pondering much over our conversation of last night, and it has suggested a question which I should wish answered, for my own guidance. You said that the highest form of inspiration could only descend by means of the operation of a conjunction of masculine and feminine elements; and that therefore its most fitting receptacle was an associated pair. But you will pardon me if I make a personal application, and ask whether those who, like yourself, are deprived of the co-operation of an earthly female associate, cannot expect to be thus inspired."

"She who was my associate on earth, and who has passed into higher conditions, is not prevented thereby from co-operating with me, in many respects far more effectually than she could otherwise have done," answered Santalba; "but this is due to the fact that during our external union we had, by long and arduous effort and ordeal, arrived at a consummation, whereby an internal and imperishable tie had been created, the mystery of which I dare not enter upon now. Hence our mental consociation differs altogether from such intercourse as you have experienced with the gross spirits of the lower regions of the unseen world, and who, in some countries, seek to communicate with man by rapping on tables, writing on slates, or even appearing in so-called materialised forms, while their human agent is a medium whom they control—a mere funnel through which they pour into the world their moral or immoral platitudes, as the case may be. I have passed through both experiences, and the difference between being a 'medium under control,' and arriving at a permanent condition of free and independent mental association, with a pure intelligence of the upper region, is greater than can be described. To be appreciated it must have been felt. It is the difference between liberty and slavery, between health and disease, between darkness and light. In the one case, one is conscious of being not merely a machine, but a machine which weakens and decays under the strain to which it is subjected. The bodily health is injured, the intellectual faculties are enfeebled, often to the point of impairing the mental balance, and life but too frequently is at last rendered miserable, by the invasion of influences which

torture both the mind and body which they
have made their abiding - place, and from
which they cannot be ejected. It is the
penalty which poor mortals pay for attempting to pry, by disorderly methods, into the
secrets of nature, which they are not meant
to penetrate.

" In the other case, on the contrary, there is a
constant sense of increased mental vigour and
bodily strength, a consciousness of moral and
intellectual freedom and spontaneity. The
individuality, instead of being suppressed, is
reinforced. With every accession of power
there flows in a rushing current of love for
the human race, and a desire to serve it.
There is no longing to pry into mysteries, because knowledge seems to ripen in the mind
more rapidly than it can be acted upon.
And knowledge which means dogma or theory,
and does not compel to practical activities, is
worthless. The benign operation of the associate intelligence is to reinforce, by means of a
subtle impregnation, the moral aspirations and
intellectual faculties of the co-worker on earth,
and this is effected with such infinite wisdom
and tenderness, that no sense is produced of

one intelligence coercing the other from without: but these derived impulses seem to spring from the man's own will-centre, so that he feels one with the being who produces them. But while experience has shown that neither the interpretations of nature's secrets by the mystics, nor the communications which have been received through spiritual mediums, have attempted to deal practically with the world's misery, we owe them this, that they have kept alive a belief in those latent forces in nature by means of which alone that misery can be successfully attacked,—they have been most useful in resisting the opposite tendency characteristic of the age, that of materialism. For if the spiritualist and the mystic wander into regions of phantasy in their attempt to construct definitions of the undefinable, and to base cosmical systems upon data which are not susceptible of scientific proof, and invent dogmas in regard to them which are of no practical utility in solving the problems of work-a-day life, the materialist, on the other hand, cuts himself off from the sources of that moral power which, if he is a good man, he most desires to possess, by refusing to investigate its dynamic properties, and the laws which appertain to them.

" Thus science alone does not enable men to regulate their emotions, because it declines to consider as within the scope of legitimate investigation, the nature of the forces by virtue of which those emotions exist. If the circumstance that the phenomena connected with the operation of the moral forces in nature do not furnish facts which are of invariable recurrence, under certain given conditions, is sufficient to exclude them from any attempt at scientific analysis, then we may look in vain to science to furnish us with any one truth which will be of the smallest benefit morally to the human race. But if its devotees will persist in limiting science to the narrow positive ground, which can never make men better, let them at all events treat with respect those who are engaged in the investigation of those vital moral phenomena, the manifestation of which in every human creature it is impossible for them to deny. For it is by the proper regulation of its vital forces that our only hope of regenerating humanity rests. At present civilised society is tossed like a shuttlecock

mainly between three classes : those who devote themselves to mystical dogmatism and
produce nothing practical ; those who devote
themselves to scientific dogmatism and produce nothing moral ; and those who, steeped
in rival theological dogmatisms,

> ' Fight like devils for conciliation,
> And hate each other for the love of God,'

and produce a very poor standard of moral
practice, but which for the present is all
that the poor world has to go upon—with
what result, the seething vice and hideous
immorality of the most populous centres
of Christendom furnish a complete illustra-
tion. So long as these three classes are un-
willing to grapple with the problems which are
involved in the sex question, and to investigate the nature of the forces which produce
depravity, with the view to the proper application of the laws inherent in those forces, and
by which they may be regulated and directed,
will they continue to run riot, in spite of
mysticism, science, or theology. Dangers of
another kind occur when these disorderly
forces chance to be diverted into an opposite
channel ; when, instead of running into vicious

excess, they propel the ignorant and super-
stitious to devotional transports, excited by
their credulous acceptance of dogmas which
have been supplied to them by their theology;
and the Church, finding itself unable to control
the emotions it has itself aroused, is compelled
to invoke the aid of the faculty.[1]

[1] The 'Times' of July 31st, 1885, gives an account of "a
remarkable outburst of religious hallucination which has been
spreading during the month past near Piacenza," where a
little girl asserted that she had seen and conversed with the
Madonna. "From that moment," continues the correspondent,
"there commenced a literal epidemic of ecstasies and visions.
While I write, more than thirty little girls declare that they
have seen, and are in direct communication with, the Madonna. . . . Hundreds and hundreds of persons are seen
labouring up the steep ascent under the burning rays of the
July sun. Some girls scramble up the bare rocks, supplicat-
ing the Virgin with loud cries to appear, until they faint with
fatigue. Recovering their senses, they say that they hear the
voice of the Madonna, while all present fall on the ground,
kissing the earth with convulsive sobs and floods of tears. A
profound impression is produced. To aggravate matters,
women known to be hysterical sing, laugh, and cry, causing
others to imitate them. While I write this, thousands are
thronging hither from the valleys of the old Duchies, from
Piedmont, from Liguria, from Lombardy. The number is
estimated at 16,000. The authorities are now interfering,
and it is high time. Several doctors who have visited the
place declare that the spread of this hallucination is likely to
assume very alarming proportions." It would be interesting
to know whether these medical men have one kind of medicine for a religious hallucination and another for a secular one.

"Meanwhile the religious instinct of the intelligent classes craves something solid to stand upon — a sure foundation upon which it can rear a new social superstructure. It has outgrown theological dogma; it rejects mystical hypothesis; it starves on scientific discovery. It demands moral fact, a demand which must remain unsatisfied so long as men continue to make arbitrary distinctions and retain antiquated definitions in regard to what they choose to call matter, soul, mind, spirit, substance, and so forth. There is one ground upon which they can all meet, and that is *force;* and one sentiment which they can all entertain for each other, and that is *charity.* With this common ground to start from, and this common sentiment to hold them together, they may hope to arrive at humane results; while facts, whether in regard to the seen or the unseen, if matters of individual experience, should be held as such by the experimenter, without any effort to force them upon the neighbour, in the firm belief and expectation that if they are true and likely to be of value to the race generally, they will be confirmed by the experience of others, until they become finally and universally recognised.

"I have been led, O sheikh, in answer to your question, into a longer digression than I intended; but the subject is one which it would require days to discuss, and I have only minutes at my disposal. I must hasten, therefore, to fulfil my commission. Here are some jewels which Amina has requested me to intrust to your safe keeping."

Thus saying, the Count produced a small box, containing a pair of diamond ear-rings and a necklace. "These stones are, as you will perceive, of immense value, though they do not nearly represent the amount which at various times Masollam has had from me. He justified the purchase of them by the virtue which he declared they possessed. On the strength of these talismanic qualities, he insisted upon Amina always wearing them. And on the ground that this was a fraudulent appropriation of money which I had given him for a different purpose, I told Amina to carry them away with her when she fled from his house. I now make them over to her, to be dealt with in the manner she sees fit. It is necessary to the work she will be called upon to do, and the position she may have to occupy, that she should feel independent financially, and these jewels will make her so. Possibly an attempt will be made to regain possession of them, and as she does not wish at present to convert them into their money value, she desires to place them in your charge."

"So much of what you have said," observed Sheikh Mohanna, as he took the jewels, "deals with social conditions with which I am unfamiliar, that I the more regret that you cannot stay longer with me now to enlighten my mind more fully in regard to the deeply interesting topics upon which you have touched; but it also convinces me that your work can never lie in this obscure Druse village. Meantime be sure that I will guard with my life, not only these diamonds, but that far more inestimable treasure, her whom you have so generously endowed with them."

"Farewell, then, for the present," said Santalba, embracing his friend; "it may be that I shall return sooner than you imagine, and find, what you expect still less, that, for a time at least, my work may lie in your remote village."

While Santalba was thus starting on his journey, furnished with a letter from Amina to her old correspondents, stating briefly the reasons which had induced her to separate herself from Masollam, the "Master" had some time before anticipated this step by an extensive correspondence, in which his disciples were warned against the woman Amina, and the serpent, in the form of Santalba, who had beguiled her. So incessant were the labours of Carabet as amanuensis, that his business in Tongsley was materially suffering from neglect. Although versed, as he had been from youth, in those arts of deceit and intrigue in which Orientals are so eminently proficient, he yet was amazed at the fertility of invention, and the audacity of misstatement, with which the combined ingenuity of his sister and her husband garnished their correspondence; while, at Masollam's dictation, he described that poor persecuted saint and his dove-like consort, he felt that whatever little moral sense he himself had ever possessed was gradually becoming so obscured, as to force him entirely to abandon any attempt to solve the riddle thus propounded. He remembered that in days gone by he had looked upon

Daoud Effendi Masollam as the wisest of
men, and upon his sister as the best of
women; and in obedience to her solicitations,
and a certain inward prompting towards good,
he had attached himself to them as a servant
of the cause which they represented. He had
himself never had that cause at heart; he had
obeyed rather the force of circumstances and
family ties than any aspiration of his own.
He sustained, therefore, no moral shock at the
revelation suggested by the correspondence in
which he was engaged : he had begun by following his sister for better, he now seemed to
be following her for worse; but after all, what
judge was he of good or bad ? These people
whom he had been accustomed to respect
above all others, thought it was all right, and
who was he, to criticise them ? He owed all
his moral training to them, and this was part
of it. Masollam was essential to the cause,
and Masollam's prestige, as a pure and holy
and gifted man, was essential to Masollam—
therefore he was serving the cause by maintaining that prestige; and besides, was not
his sister wealthy, and was he not in a
sense dependent upon her ? and how could he
better ensure his own comfort and happiness

than by blind and supple obedience? So he contentedly scribbled and posted packets of lies; until at last the day came when Masollam, turning to Tigranuhe, said, "That, I think, completes the list. No doubt the answers will come pouring in before very long; but we shall be able to escape them by returning to Damascus. This detestable climate chills me to the marrow; and my associations with The Turrets are not so agreeable that I wish to linger here. You still think that it would be better to go in pursuit of Amina than of Sebastian?"

"Distinctly," said Madame Masollam; "and for two reasons. In the first place, we do not know where Sebastian is; and we have discovered that Amina has returned with Santalba to Syria. In the second place, if we found Sebastian, the whole position of matters is so changed since his marriage, and our relations with his uncle are so unfriendly, that it would be very difficult, even in the absence of Santalba, to carry out our original intention with regard to him; and we should be exposed at any moment to interruption by the inopportune arrival of the Count. Besides, I believe Clareville is with him. No; we must allow events to develop in that direction."

"But do you feel sure we shall not meet Santalba in Syria, if he has gone there with Amina?" asked Masollam, nervously.

"No; it is impossible for him to stay there. He is more likely to visit some of those friends to whom we have been writing; but he will find that we have been too quick for him."

"Well, then, give me pen and ink, and I will myself write to Charles Hartwright, to tell him that he is welcome to return and reoccupy The Turrets at his convenience. I thus make him a present of the unfulfilled lease: it will be a civility which costs nothing, and may be of service to us later."

So saying, the old man wrote a letter couched in most friendly language to his landlord; and the same day Carabet, to the surprise of Tongsley, announced his intention of closing up his business. Within less than a week from that time, the mysterious Orientals, whose presence in that north-country town had been a matter of no little gossip and wonderment to its inhabitants, vanished from the scene; and a month later, Mr and Mrs Hartwright, with their sons and Laura, once more entered into peaceful possession of The Turrets.

CHAPTER VI.

SHEIKH SHIBLEY MAKES A PROPOSAL OF MARRIAGE.

IT was not unnatural that the anomalous
position which Amina occupied among her own
people, should give rise to some discussion
among the members of her family; and these,
if we include those of more remote degree,
were by no means despicable in numbers.
Although women are held in far higher estimation among the Druses than among the
Moslems, and many of them even rise to the
rank of Okâl, or Initiated, and have been
known to exercise great influence, they are
still regarded as inferior beings, and, as a rule,
have but little voice in shaping their own
destiny. A Druse woman is never permitted
to marry a man of another religion; and if a

Druse man should marry a Moslem or Christian woman, an almost unknown event, she
is bound to become a Druse. The fact that
a girl born of Druse parents should not be a
Druse also by religion, was a novelty so un-
precedented, that it formed the subject of
several weighty discussions at those meetings of sheikhs, who, coming from other villages, form secret councils in their church or
khalweh in which the affairs, political and
religious, of the nation are discussed; and
it required all the great influence of Sheikh
Mohanna to stave off a decision which compelled his niece to give in a formal adhesion
to the Druse faith, in the terms prescribed
by her religion. He explained that, being a
person of great intelligence, she could not be
expected blindly to adopt a creed involving such profound mysteries, without being
instructed therein. That naturally, having
been brought up in entire ignorance of the
most elementary principles of the Druse religion, some time would be required for her
education, and this Sheikh Mohanna under-
took to furnish; a task, he said, which would
be rendered more easy from the fact that she

had never belonged to any of the existing forms of religion, and that she had therefore none of those prejudices to overcome, which are inseparable from dogmatic creeds. It was therefore agreed that, so far as the religious question was concerned, she should be left in peace, until Sheikh Mohanna announced that she had completed her theological studies, and was ready to give in her adhesion to the faith of her people. There was another question, however, which the old sheikh saw looming in the near future, and which caused him considerable perturbation of mind. He was at no difficulty to account for the frequent visits of her cousin Shibley, whose growing passion for Amina her cold and distant treatment only seemed to inflame, and he was therefore quite prepared one day for a formal demand from the young sheikh for the hand of his niece.

"You have already an affectionate and devoted wife, who has borne you three children," said Sheikh Mohanna, in a tone of mild remonstrance.

"She is no longer my wife; I divorced her yesterday," answered Sheikh Shibley. "Think you I would come here and ask for your niece to wife if I was still a married man ?"

"Then you have been unduly precipitate, and have parted yourself for ever from one whom you will find it difficult, if not impossible, to replace. Dismiss the thought at once from your mind, that your wishes in regard to Amina can ever be gratified, at least while I am alive," pursued the old sheikh, somewhat sternly. "I have already conversed with her on the subject, foreseeing this contingency—believe me, in no unfriendly spirit towards you—and she has distinctly, and in the most positive terms, assured me that under no circumstances could she ever be your wife. As I am determined neither to coerce her myself, nor to see her coerced in this matter by others, you will perceive that the marriage you desire is impossible, and you will best consult your own happiness by giving up all idea of it."

By an immense effort of will, Shibley suppressed the rage with which he felt convulsed, and after a pause, during which he regained his self-control so far as to be able to mutter with a sneer, "Be it so, O sheikh; I can

reconcile myself to the disappointment the
more easily, since she is still an unbeliever,"
he turned away and rode gloomily home,
more determined than ever to carry his point.

Sheikh Mohanna remained for some time in
deep meditation; he then rose and went to
the women's apartments, where he found his
sister Sada busily engaged in the domestic
operation of boiling carob syrup.

" Where is Amina?" he asked.

" She has gone to see Afifi, who is danger-
ously ill of fever," replied Sada; and the
sheikh proceeded in search of his niece to
the village.

Afifi was the only daughter of the Khateeb,
a lovely girl of eighteen, who, from the
moment she had first seen Amina, had been
struck with an admiration which had speedily
ripened into a devoted attachment. Indeed,
during the few weeks which had elapsed
since the arrival of the late sheikh's daughter,
she had succeeded in winning the hearts
of the whole of the female population; while
the men were unwillingly obliged to admit
to themselves that she compelled a sentiment of deference and respect such as they

had never before accorded to a woman, and for the growth of which they were somewhat at a loss to account. She had adopted the national costume ; had made herself personally conversant with the domestic affairs of each household ; had afforded pecuniary assistance to the poorest families ; was unwearied in her attendance on, and devotion to, the sick, and most successful in her treatment of them. She was already by these means acquiring an influence, which she turned to good account by acting as a peacemaker in the family disputes which were constantly arising, and in which the whole village was in the habit of taking sides. She distributed her favours equally between the two leading families, whose feud had for years divided the village, which she was the better able to do, as her own position was superior to both, and it was in the house of one of these she was now ministering. It was built in a courtyard entered by rather an imposing stone gateway, above which had been constructed a square chamber, which was the one appropriated by the Khateeb to the numerous guests he was in the habit of receiving from the neighbour-

ing villages. On one side of the court was
a pen for goats, and a verandah affording
stabling accommodation; on the other, a mill
for crushing olives. This was under cover,
and was a somewhat elaborate apparatus,
which differed in no degree probably from
that used in the country from the earliest
times. Here was the huge circular bottom
stone, about eight feet in diameter, with a rim
six inches high, which is traversed by an
upright stone of smaller dimensions, the exact
counterparts of which are to be found among
the stones of the most ancient ruins. They
are worked by a huge upright shaft, from
which extends a lateral beam, and to it is
attached the necessary horse-power.

In one corner of this yard stands a small
isolated construction, which contains only a
circular pit about four feet deep and two feet
in diameter. It is the domestic oven, and
sitting near it are two women engaged in
baking bread. A crackling wood-fire is blaz-
ing at the bottom, so that the smooth sides
are heated up to a high point. Between the
women is a circular cushion, about a foot in
diameter and two inches thick. They in turn

take a large handful of the kneaded and moist-
ened flour, and dexterously throwing it from
hand to hand, flatten it out until it is in the
form of a pancake the size of the cushion,
upon which they rapidly spread it, and, with a
quick skilful movement, slap it on the side of
the oven, with a force which spreads it out to
a wafer at least eighteen inches in diameter.
Here it sticks for a minute or two, when it is
pulled off and piled in a heap. The women
engaged in this operation perform it with in-
credible skill and rapidity; and the result of
their labours, if eaten as soon as it is baked,
is by no means unpalatable.

The actual residence of the Khateeb occu-
pies the fourth side of the court in which
these varied industries are in progress, front-
ing the main gateway, and consists of two
large apartments, which are divided by a row
of arches connected at their base by a low
wall, from which spring in each room three
arches spanning it transversely; upon these
are laid the rough logs of mountain wood
which form the flat roof, and which in their
turn are covered with a thick layer of tempered mud. These logs are blackened beneath

by the smoke of the winter fires, which are
built in the centre of the rooms, the only
outlets for the smoke being the doors and
windows. In the corners, in the angles made
by the arches, on every available space on
the wall, are projecting constructions built of
mud, ornamented with raised patterns and
quaint devices of the same material, which
serve the purpose of cupboards and granaries;
and there are little trap-doors in the latter,
through which the grain, which has been
poured in above, can be allowed to issue at
will. Besides which there are projecting
ledges or shelves, also ornamented; and the
guns, pistols, and other weapons belonging to
the male members of the household, are hung
in picturesque confusion side by side with
sieves, circular dining-mats of coloured straw,
cooking utensils, and other articles of domestic
necessity. One large recess is set apart for the
reception of mattresses, coverlets, and cushions,
which are heaped in it in a pile reaching from
the floor almost to the roof. At night these
are all pulled out and spread over the floor,
thus affording as much sleeping accommodation as there is area; from which it will ap-

pear that, if there is not much furniture in one sense of the word—for bedsteads, tables, and chairs are conspicuous by their absence— the walls are abundantly garnished with all that contributes to the comfort of Druse home-life. But there is one feature in the internal economy of the establishment which, if it is the least agreeable to the stranger, is the most characteristic. On the further sides of both the apartments I have been describing run rows of mangers on a level with the floor. The more valuable animals, kept there for the sake of greater security and convenience for winter feeding, actually occupy the same room with the family, though the level of the floor upon which they stand is about two feet lower. In the summer, when the cattle are for the most part away, these mangers are a convenience both to babies and foreigners. They serve as a cradle to the one, and as a seat for the other, as it is more comfortable to sit on the edge of a manger, and put your feet into it, than to tuck them under you on a mat. But even in summer these sociable stables are always to some extent used; and at the moment when Sheikh Mohanna entered

the house of the Khateeb, the apartment occupied by the invalid was also tenanted by a
mare and her foal, two cows and a donkey,
a lean cat, and a number of long - legged
chickens, while he might have counted no
fewer than twenty - four men, women, and
children crowded round the mattress on the
floor, which formed the couch of the sick girl.
Amina was remonstrating at the moment of
his entrance with the girl's mother, who was
giving vent to her feelings in a loud wail,
which was occasionally echoed by some of the
other women, while her father was endeavour-
ing to rouse his daughter to consciousness by
bawling her name in her ear. To add to the
din, several babies were crying; a strange
cur had entered the yard, and given rise to a
furious remonstrance of barking on the part
of its recognised canine proprietors; and the
donkey, finding the moment propitious, swelled
the uproar by a sympathetic bray.

On seeing the sheikh, Amina rushed to meet
him with streaming eyes.

"O uncle," she exclaimed, "I am so glad
you have come! I am quite in despair. If
Afifi dies, she will have been killed by those

people ; she is at a most critical point, and her only chance is perfect quiet, and air that is not poisoned by a crowd that shuts off every pure breath from her. Do, please, exert your authority. Try and clear the room of the different variety of animals that infest it. I believe I could answer for her recovery if I only had a fair chance. I have one of Madame Masollam's medicines here, which I am sure would exactly meet the case. You know what marvellous instinct she had for treating all kinds of disease, and how skilled she was in the use of herbs and simples. She taught me a great deal; and I have got a collection of most of her remedies, besides many others that are well known and in general use. The people admit that I have used them already with the greatest success ; but, because Afifi is the village favourite, and they think she is going to die, their distress is so great that they will listen to no reason : the Khateeb will kill her, if you do not drag him away from her ear."

It was not without difficulty that even Sheikh Mohanna, with his great authority, succeeded in clearing the room and producing some kind of quiet ; and finding that Amina

was determined to remain with her patient,·
not only for the rest of the day but throughout
the night, he insisted that his own presence
was also necessary to secure her the conditions
she required.

So absorbed was she in her tender cares,
that the old man felt that the moment was
not an opportune one to broach the subject
which had brought him to her side; but as he
silently watched her flitting about the sick-
room like a ministering angel, her natural
grace seemed so much enhanced in his eyes by
the costume with which he was familiar, that
he felt that he could not blame Shibley for
having fallen the victim to a passion which
a being so lovely was so well calculated to
inspire.   And indeed Amina's beauty was of a
type which corresponded admirably with her
own national costume.   Her outer garment
consisted of a dark-blue robe, trimmed with
wide bands of red satin, the short light sleeves
of which were cut above the elbow; it was
open all down the front, so as to leave visible
the semi-transparent chemise, which, richly
embroidered with silk round the neck, and
trimmed with strips of a heavy white, con-

cealed as with a tunic the loose trousers which
descended to the ankles, round which they
were confined. The white sleeves of the
chemise, widely pointed, escaped from the
shorter ones of the outer robe, leaving the arm
bare to the elbow; a scarf of bright scarlet
was wound round the waist, above which,
and below the bosom, the folds of the outer
robe were caught together by a button, thus
giving the effect of that double girdle often
represented in ancient classical costume. The
head-dress consisted of a long white cloth,
with the centre of one edge drawn low upon
the forehead, its two ends hanging down the
back to the heels; bound round the head by a
wide fillet of brightly variegated colours, it
resembled somewhat that worn by the ancient
Egyptians, and its simplicity accorded well
with the regular outline of the features of the
wearer.

"My beloved child," said the old skeikh, as
Amina, after having prepared and given her
patient some medicine, and arranged her pillows, came and seated herself on the cushion
by her uncle's side, "you are wearing yourself
out in your labours for your people; you allow

yourself no time for rest, or," he added with a
sly glance at her, "for your studies into the
mysteries of our religion."

"These are the mysteries of my religion,"
replied Amina, as she pointed to the sick
girl. "Find me a cure for the diseases of
body and of spirit, and you have solved the
only mystery I desire to penetrate. That
girl's illness is not purely physical. She
is sick at heart — I feel it here," and she
pressed her hand upon her own side. "Do
you know why I am successful in dealing
with disease? because I nearly always feel the
patients' symptoms in myself. Not always.
If I don't, it is a sign to me that for some
reason I can do nothing for them, or am not
intended to. For instance, the other day,
Shibley, having heard that I had some skill in
the healing art, came to me, with a description of violent pains which he felt in his side,
accompanied with shortness of breath ; but I
could feel nothing of it, though I held his
hand for some time, and sought to open myself
to some perception of his malady. So I was
obliged to tell him I could do nothing for him."

"Perhaps the real reason was that he had

nothing the matter with him—at least, nothing that medicine could cure," replied the sheikh, with a smile of some meaning.

"I told him he ought rather to consult you than me," continued Amina, simply. "On all sides I hear stories of the marvellous cures which you used to accomplish, and regrets expressed that you refuse any longer to make use of your exceptional gifts. Will you tell me your reason, uncle?"

"I came to perceive that my perceptions were not to be relied upon, because they were the result of certain organic conditions, which were in themselves disorderly. I induced them, by long periods of fasting, during which I repeatedly fell into trances, when powerful influences would take possession of me, and afterwards project through my touch a healing virtue; but as during these trances I was naturally unable to choose between these influences, or control their action, I began to discover that, while my touch was in some instances beneficial, in others it was pernicious, and this led me to doubt whether I was in the right path, and for many reasons, which it is not neces-

sary for me now to enter upon, I came to the
conclusion that I was not acting in accordance
with the divine will in the matter, and that
these experiences were permitted to convince
me of that fact."

"In the absence of scientific knowledge to
help us, the whole subject, indeed, is one surrounded with danger and difficulty," returned
Amina; "and I have made up my mind,
whenever I return to Europe, to enter as a
student of medicine, and go through the whole
course necessary to qualify myself to become
a medical practitioner; for I quite agree with
you that such powers as you possessed are too
inconstant, and do not belong to the means
lawfully at the disposal of man."

"It seems nevertheless strange," said Sheikh
Mohanna, with a sigh, "to reject the resources
which these profounder spiritual knowledges
and potencies supply, and to descend for your
wisdom and your remedial agents to the low
level of ordinary science."

"Don't suppose," interrupted Amina, quickly,
"that I regard the highest established results
of medical science as containing more than a
part—if you will, but a small part—of the re-

quisite information in dealing with disease; but it is an essential part. The study of human anatomy, of pharmaco-dynamics, and of therapeutics, is one thing; the principle of diagnosis is a totally different one. So long as a gulf is allowed to separate—both in the minds of patients and their medical advisers — the physical from the moral organism, so long will diagnoses, which are based upon the hypothetical existence of this gulf, be imperfect. And yet," she added, "in practice, even the most materialistic of practitioners will often be forced to do violence to his theories in this respect. Take, for instance, the case of a girl who is pining to death under the influence of moral starvation, caused by unrequited affection; the physician will prescribe, not a drug, but that moral atmosphere which the presence of the beloved object can only supply."

As she thus spoke, Amina was interrupted by the low moaning of her patient, as she moved restlessly on her mattress. "If I am not much mistaken," she said, "here is a case in point."

"And here," said Sheikh Mohanna, taking his niece's hand, and looking gravely into her large soft eyes, " is another. Only in this case the sexes are reversed."

" What do you mean, uncle ? "

" I mean that, whether Shibley's symptoms were real or assumed when he applied to you as a physician, he is at this moment morally diseased, his whole nature unhinged, by his love for you. He has just been with me, to endeavour to obtain my consent to your union. I told him that I had already spoken to you on the subject, and that your feeling in the matter had been so clearly expressed, as to leave me no alternative but to refuse that consent absolutely. On which he left me, with a smooth tongue, but an eye that betrayed the passion that lurked behind it, and which meant mischief."

" What you tell me grieves, but it does not surprise me. I was prepared for something of the sort by a conversation which I had with mother, on the subject, this morning. A very painful one."

" How so ? "

" It is the first difference I have had with her, and she finally became very violent. She insists that I shall accept Shibley, and declares that from the moment she heard that I was living she had destined me for him, and that it is not a matter upon which I have any right of choice. She tells me that she has even gone so far as to promise me to him, and to recommend him to divorce his present wife."

"He has followed her advice, and already done so," said the sheikh.

In the burst of her indignation at this intelligence, Amina failed to hear a low quick exclamation which issued from the lips of the invalid, as her uncle imparted it.

"And these are my people!" she exclaimed bitterly; "and this is one of the mysteries of their religion, of which, no doubt, in due course of time, I am to have personal experience! Uncle, you must send at once for that poor abandoned wife and her three little ones. Henceforth they must belong to me and be at my charge—unless, indeed, Shibley can be forced to take her back."

"That is quite impossible—it is strictly prohibited. He can never, even in the whole course of his life, speak to her again; and should they see each other at a distance, they must turn aside to avoid meeting."

"And she loved him ?"

"With all her heart, from the time she was a child. She has never had a thought but for Shibley."

"Then," said Amina, sadly, "she is a fit subject for the mysteries of *my* religion, and I will instruct her in them."

"I understand your feelings, my child ; and, believe me, I sympathise with them. As you must know by this time, I am but a Druse in name. I have long repudiated, in the secrecy of my own conscience, that religion of which at one time I was one of the most learned expounders; for as I advanced into its more hidden mysteries, I saw that they led to a negation of the facts of my own inner consciousness, and of truths which had been revealed to it; but my people are not prepared to receive these truths, and I should only do harm by exciting their suspicions in any way. Therefore we must act in this matter with judgment and caution, concealing as much as may be our real designs, for this is the habit of Druses—and in certain cases it is not only expedient but lawful. Instil, therefore, those purer principles of morality which you desire to impart with subtlety, and not in a manner calculated to rouse existing prejudices or excite suspicion, while you may still be supposed to be receiving instruction from me, as in many things, in fact, you are. And as for this Shibley matter, rest in peace. I will watch over you, and protect you from him. Avoid discussing the subject further with your mother, who will, nevertheless, violently oppose your taking charge of the wife and children; but to this I will make her submit."

"Afifi's whole condition has changed!" interrupted Amina, suddenly starting up and going to the girl. "Come here, uncle."

The sheikh approached.

"See," continued Amina in a low tone, "into what a tranquil sleep she has fallen. Feel her pulse—how calmly it beats! The crisis has passed, or rather it was never actually reached. It has been averted by a life-current which has poured in from some unknown quarter. All the moral pain has gone. The girl is cured!" she exclaimed delightedly. "Help me to get down another mattress and some pillows. I will spread them here and go to sleep by her side.

There is no occasion for me to watch any longer, or for you to stay, dear uncle."

Sheikh Mohanna stood for some moments gazing at the girl in deep thought.

"You are right, my child," he said at length. "There is no need of my staying; but before I leave you I will tell you the unknown quarter from which that life-current came. Afifi was not so unconscious as we supposed her to be. She overheard you say that you would never marry Shibley; she overheard me say that he had divorced his wife; and—she loves him!"

CHAPTER VII.

WHEN GREEK MEETS GREEK.

WHILE Sheikh Mohanna and Amina had been watching by the side of the Khateeb's sick daughter, Sheikh Shibley was riding gloomily home, revolving in his mind a project for the violent abduction of his beautiful cousin. He was sure of the co-operation of her mother and of many members of her family; but he foresaw that the preliminary arrangements must be conducted with the greatest caution and secrecy, and might involve the expenditure of more ready money than he had in hand. He therefore determined to raise the necessary amount upon part of his landed property; and to this end it was needful that he should visit a friend of the Jewish persuasion who was resident at Damascus, and often resorted to by the *fella-*

heen in their financial difficulties. Now this
man was an old acquaintance of Carabet's,
who, having arrived at Damascus with the
Masollams only a few days before, happened
to be in his friend's shop at the moment when
Shibley entered it. In the course of the preliminary compliments which were being inter-
changed, Carabet's quick ear caught the name
of Teraya, which he knew to be Amina's native village, and where the Jew had some ac-
quaintances whom he was inquiring after—
among others, Sheikh Mohanna. As soon,
therefore, as coffee was introduced, and the
financial subject was entered upon, Carabet
took part in the conversation, finally offering
to supply Sheikh Shibley with the sum needed
on easier terms than he was likely elsewhere
to obtain, and making an appointment with
him for the following morning at the same
place. On Shibley's leaving, Carabet arranged
with his friend that the latter should have a
commission on the transaction, and particu-
larly warned him not to mention Masollam's
name to the Druse.

"Truly the gods befriend us!" remarked
Carabet to his sister, when he hurried back

to her with the news. " I happened to turn into old Isaac's, knowing that he was acquainted with that part of the country, to see what I could pick up with regard to the position of affairs at Teraya, when who should come in but a Druse sheikh of a neighbouring village, who it seems is in want of money to pay his taxes with, and who is a cousin of Amina's? for when I asked him whether he had ever known Sheikh Sâleh Zedaan of Teraya, he drew himself up with an air and replied, ' I am his cousin's son, Sheikh Shibley Zedaan.' I therefore made an appointment with him for to-morrow, when I will bring him here, promising him the money at twenty-five per cent, which is five per cent less than he can get elsewhere, provided the security is satisfactory."

" Did you not ask him for news of Amina?" asked Masollam.

" I left all such inquiries for you, O Master! fearing I might excite his curiosity or be indiscreet in my questions. I even took precautions to conceal your presence here."

" You did quite right, brother," said Tigranuhe, with a glance of contempt at the old

man; "and I think," she added, turning upon
him sharply, "you will do well when he comes
to be equally guarded; in fact, excepting in
the pure matter of business, you had better
not interfere, but leave the extracting of the
information to me."

This was said in a tone of scornful authority, which suggested that the relations of
the pair had undergone a marked change since
our first acquaintance with them at The Turrets; and indeed there was evidence of this
in Masollam's countenance as well as in his
manner. Those singular facial transforma-
tions had become more rare and less marked;
the sudden manifestations of youthful vigour
were less frequent; the eyes seemed to have
lost their power of emitting fierce flashing
glances, and to be growing dim and sullen.
If the vital fuel was not perceptibly burning
lower, it had ceased, apparently, to show those
reinforcements of combustible material, which
had blazed forth periodically in the looks and
tones and gestures of the man, and from the
fiery glow of which he had derived his highest
inspirations. Thus the forces to which he had
owed his remarkable powers seemed to be slowly

abandoning him, and his real character, which those forces had suppressed, began to betray itself, more especially in his relations with his wife. A growing hatred of her was gradually taking possession of his soul; and with the consciousness of his own increasing weakness, there entered a sentiment of distrust and suspicion of her every word and act. He became haunted by a mortal dread of the consequences to which her cupidity and her ambitions might lead her,—for in his recent correspondence with his disciples she had compelled him to associate her with himself as his equal in spiritual authority. She had, moreover, in many instances, assumed the right to give directions, and to carry on a correspondence of her own, consulting him nominally, it is true, but only *pro formâ*. His own spiritual pride was so overweening, that to submit tamely to this usurpation of a supreme authority seemed more than he could endure, while, on the other hand, he was convinced that, should he rebel against it, he might incur serious risk, since his death would have the double merit of leaving her without a rival, as supreme priestess and prophetess of the sys-

tem which he had founded, and of putting
her in possession of all his property. So
deeply versed was she in the knowledge of
the properties of herbs and medicaments, and
so familiar in theory with the art, so much
practised in the East, of " removing" human
inconveniences in a quiet and unostentatious
manner, that he shuddered when he thought
of the simple contingency upon which his
existence depended. A prey to these appre-
hensions, his life was rendered miserable ; and
while he was constantly revolving schemes
whereby he might counteract the designs
of his female associate, his manner to her
became more cringing and propitiatory, just
in the degree in which he feared her.
With all this, his passion for Amina was as
strong as ever. Tigranuhe, on the other hand,
astonished her brother by a growing development of faculty and assumption of power :
she no longer disguised, when they were
alone, her contempt for Masollam's weakness
and timidity, and read him like an open
book.

Such were the relations which subsisted between these singular beings at the time when

Sheikh Shibley, came to seek financial assistance. On the following morning, Carabet met him according to appointment, and soon after, Shibley found himself ushered into the handsome, marble-paved, open court, which was the chief ornament of Masollam's mansion in Damascus. Not that the richly divaned and heavily carpeted chambers left anything to desire in the way of expensive decoration and elaborate oriental design ; but the court, with its plashing fountains, and orange-trees, and scented flowers, was the striking feature, and the Druse chief, who was not accustomed to such magnificence, paused a moment in admiration of it. Indeed, many of Masollam's disciples, who had at various times come to pick up learning at the Master's feet, and had expected to find a self-denying recluse, living in the utmost simplicity, were amazed and somewhat shocked at the evidences of luxury and extravagance by which they found themselves surrounded, until they were accounted for by the plausible reasons which Masollam had ever ready at his tongue's end. Here a servant met them, who whispered a few words to Carabet.

"I find that my brother-in-law, who is associated with me in business," explained the latter, "has been unexpectedly detained on some important matters at the Serai, and will be here presently. Will you have the kindness to enter the divan and wait for him?"

As punctuality is not an Eastern virtue, Shibley did not regard this as any hardship, and while he was consoling himself with a nargileh, Tigranuhe entered.

"This is my sister," said Carabet. "When she heard from me that you belonged to the great family of Zedaan, her heart was made glad, for the dearest friend she has in the world—one who has been to her as her own daughter—belongs to that family."

Shibley made a graceful salute, and looked at the lady for further explanation.

"My brother speaks truly," she remarked. "If, as he tells me, you are indeed the son of Sheikh Sâleh Zedaan's cousin, you must know the strange history of Amina, the daughter of the sheikh?"

"I have heard it from her own lips."

"And did she not tell you of Daoud Effendi Masollam and his wife?"

Shibley's heart gave a bound; here was a sudden and unlooked-for combination of circumstances indeed. He had heard of the Masollams from Sada—a strange confused account, from which he could gather nothing as to the reasons which had induced them to keep her so long in confinement and in ignorance of her daughter's presence, or of the real causes of their flight. He had conceived of them as rich, mysterious, and designing people, whose motives he had no means of fathoming; and he was the more perplexed, because in his endeavours to obtain further information on the subject, first from Amina herself, and then from Sheikh Mohanna, they had each of them changed the subject, and had manifested the strongest disinclination to return to it. Under these circumstances, in his uncertainty of the ground upon which he was treading, he determined to exercise the greatest caution, and the Druse way of doing this is to prevaricate.

"She has told me of friends she had lived with all the years we supposed her dead. One, indeed, called Girius Bey, came with her; but she did not mention the names of others, or, if she did, I have forgotten them."

"Know then, O sheikh, that I have been to her as a mother, and that she believed me in fact to be her mother, ever since she was brought to me by Girius Bey as a baby twenty-five years ago; and that the principal reason which has brought us back from Europe, where we have been recently living, was to see the beloved child again."

"I can well imagine how you must have loved her," he said; "she is, indeed, a pearl among women. Although she has not been with us many weeks, and I have seen but little of her, as I do not reside in her village, I have seen enough to assure me of that. It must have been a severe trial to you to part with one you loved so much."

"A terrible trial indeed," said Tigranuhe, drawing a corner of the veil which formed part of her head-dress to her eyes, and wiping away an imaginary tear; "but not so terrible as the ingratitude from which we have suffered, the misconstruction which has been placed upon our motives, and the falsehoods which have been circulated in regard to our acts. I fear that my husband's dear old friend Sheikh Mohanna, whom he has always held in the highest esteem, has had his mind poisoned against us. I do not charge the dear child with any of these things, nor that simple and worthy woman her mother, who, of course, could not understand that in a country like England, where religious fanaticism runs high, we were obliged to conceal her for her own safety. It was that fiend in human shape, Girius Bey, who, when he heard that we had found that her mother was still living, instead of allowing us to send Amina to her at once, was the cause of our bringing both mother and daughter to England."

" What was his object in that ? "

" To marry Amina, to be sure," said Tigranuhe, unblushingly.

In Shibley's involuntary start at receiving this unexpected piece of information, the woman read his secret, and she rubbed her hands softly together with satisfaction as she saw the ally he was likely to prove.

A thousand circumstances rushed to Shibley's mind in confirmation of this statement. The undisguised affection with which Amina always spoke of Girius Bey, and which she had taken no pains to conceal during the time

he had seen them together; the influence
which he perceived the foreigner exercised
over Sheikh Mohanna; and the refusal of the
latter to coerce Amina, whose affections he
was now sure were already engaged, or she
could never have resisted his own attractions,
—all proved the truth of Madame Masollam's
assertion.

"But why, if he wanted to marry her, did
he need the presence of her mother?" he
asked.

"He did not need it; but we had pledged
Sada to restore her to her daughter, so we
were obliged to take her. Moreover, we suspected Girius of a selfish motive, though he
pretended it was necessary that Amina should
come to England in order that he might settle
some money on her; and we thought the presence of Sada might prove a restraint upon
him, as indeed it did. I wish," added Tigranuhe, with a sigh, "I could see the dear
girl removed from the clutch of that unbelieving foreign dog, and safely married to
one of her own people."

Shibley glanced at her suspiciously. Was
not she, from his point of view, as foreign and

unbelieving as the man she was reviling? Had not she, too, a game to play? and could not he read her secret? for with the morbid consciousness of a lover, he began to perceive that she had read his.

"And did he settle the money he intended upon her?" he inquired.

"He relieved himself from that intention, if he ever had it, by compelling her to steal some valuable jewels that belonged to me."

Shibley's eyes kindled for a moment, and then he darted a glance at the Armenian, which she received with a responsive flash. And these two very clever people knew at once what each read in the eye of the other. In the glow of the Druse's, Tigranuhe saw passion; in the glitter of hers, Shibley read avarice. And to each occurred the same reflection, that, dexterously used, each could be made to serve the other's ends.

"Girius has probably converted them into money," said Shibley.

"Possibly; or possibly Amina may have them with her now. I have been thinking of visiting Teraya, in order to find this out, and also for the purpose of regaining my

influence over the beloved child. It would
need but twenty-four hours together for me
to induce her to banish her false lover from
her heart, and to substitute for him one who
was worthy of her. At the same time, my
husband could use his influence with Sheikh
Mohanna, which is great, in the same direction, and show him the impropriety of allowing the present relations to continue between
his niece and this foreigner, if there should be
one of her own people seeking an alliance with
her ; while, if it should become necessary, you
could bring the whole question up for consideration upon the first occasion of a meeting
of the Okâls of your religion, as it is a matter
in which an important principle is involved."

Tigranuhe's suggestions fell very pleasantly
on Shibley's ears. Certainly they presented
many advantages over the rough-and-ready
method of the night assault on Sheikh Mohanna's residence which he had proposed to
himself, and which, even if it were successful,
must involve him in serious feuds and trouble
later. He felt a strength and comfort in the
bold and subtle intelligence of his newly found
ally ; and thinking he would like to talk

matters out more openly than was possible in the presence of Carabet, he glanced uneasily at the Armenian.

"Brother," said Tigranuhe, detecting the movement, "go and see whether the Master has returned from the Serai"—accompanying the words with a look which Carabet interpreted without difficulty to mean, "Go away, stay away, and keep Masollam away."

"Now," she continued, when her brother had vanished, "there is no danger of interruption: and to give you an evidence of my sincerity, and save time, I will speak frankly. You have come here to borrow money. It is unnecessary; you can have it without borrowing, provided we come to an understanding in regard to our mutual interests. My diamonds I believe to be at Teraya. I am in communication with all the diamond merchants in Europe in a position to purchase such stones, and they are few, and should have been informed ere this had they been offered for sale. Not being with them, I am convinced they are in Amina's keeping. Girius loves her too well to deprive her of them. Were it not for her fear of offending him, I

should only have to ask Amina for them, and
she would give them to me. As it is, I am
prepared to pay any one well who will restore
them to me; and more than that, if he desires,
as a still greater reward, the possession of her
whom he deprives of these gems, I will secure
him the prize he covets."

"I thank you, O lady, for speaking thus
openly; for, as you rightly judge, I am he who
covets the prize, which is to me worth gems of
infinite price. But how can you assure her to
me? for I fear me that she is one who will
submit to no pressure, unless her heart also
consents."

"Leave that to me, my son," responded
Tigranuhe, assuming an air of maternal
benevolence. "I have not reared the maiden
from infancy, and studied the properties of
the gifts with which nature teems, without
having at my command potions of such exquisite and delicate virtue, that they can be
applied with certain effect where the character
of the temperament is known; and I know
Amina's temperaments—I can play upon her
passions as upon the strings of an instrument."

Shibley listened to this statement with a certain credulous wonder: it never occurred to him to doubt it.

"Be it so," he said. "I perceive indeed that you are a woman of knowledge and of skill, and I place myself under your guidance."

"Return, then, to Teraya, assure yourself not only that the diamonds are there, but also where they are kept. Then return here with all the information you have been able to obtain, and we will fully discuss our plans. Above all, do not breathe to a living soul that you have seen us in Damascus."

Shibley hesitated a moment, and then said, not without a shade of embarrassment—

"It is well, O lady, to have affairs of this sort clearly defined. If, through my instrumentality, you obtain possession of the jewels, I would inquire, how much money do you propose to give me? For although I am obeying your instructions in this matter for the sake of Amina, and not for the sake of money, and although I place every confidence in your assurances that you will win for me the love of her I desire as a wife, still the greatest skill avails not against destiny; and

if by chance, after winning you your gems, I
lost my bride, I should need compensation
and consolation indeed."

"And you shall have it. If you recover for
me my jewels, and I obtain for you your
bride, I will give you as a marriage present
fifty thousand piastres. And if you recover
for me my jewels, and I do not win Amina
for you, then I will engage to double that
sum, which will furnish you with sufficient to
obtain possession of her in another, though
perhaps a more violent way."

"It is well," said Shibley; and taking from
his girdle a brass inkstand, containing also
some reed-pens and a small roll of paper,
with which he had come prepared for a
very different negotiation, he wrote in a few
words the substance of the agreement, which
he presented to Tigranuhe for signature.
That lady was somewhat taken aback by the
prompt and business-like character of this
proceeding; and as she slowly perused the
document, she sought in vain for an excuse,
under cover of which she might avoid com-
mitting herself in writing to so strange a
compact. She felt, however, that any hesita-

tion would rouse the suspicions of the Druse; and knowing the inveterate tendency to mistrust which characterises the race, she signed her name in Arabic characters, below which the sheikh stamped his own, with his brass signet.

"I am sorry," she said, when he had done this, "that my husband has not been here to give further validity to this document, the more especially as I fear, since he has not returned yet, that he may now be detained for many hours longer; but if you like to leave it with me, I will obtain his signature." Madame Masollam thus hoped to gain possession of the contract.

"It is unnecessary," replied Shibley; "I will bring back a copy for both to sign, as I am well aware that this is of but trifling value, but it will be useful as a memorandum. And now, as you have given up the hope of your husband returning soon, and as I would start with as little delay as possible on my journey home, I will bid you farewell, O lady."

"May God prosper you, and grant you a safe return!" ejaculated Madame Masollam, piously. "A cunning man and a treacherous," she mused, as she watched the Druse striding across the courtyard. "Safer perhaps as an enemy than a friend : at all events, one to be narrowly watched."

"What a sweet revenge it would be," she muttered, "if I could, whether by fraud or force, place Amina in the embrace of this semi-barbarian! What a revenge on the 'Master,' on Santalba, on that haughty English aristocrat Clareville, and above all, on herself! There is no other woman, either in this world or the other, that I am afraid of; and each time that I meet her in my trances, in the inner region, her powers have increased, and her guardian spirits have drawn more closely round her; but the battle must be fought out on the terrestrial plane." She closed her eyes and remained motionless for a few moments, and then murmured again softly to herself—"There is no longer room for doubt. The crisis for us both has arrived. And it is now a struggle between us, perhaps of life or death."

CHAPTER VIII.

CONSPIRACY AND TREACHERY.

WHEN Sheikh Mohanna had assured Amina that he would have Shibley's divorced wife at once brought from the village of the latter to his own house, he was aware that difficulties might arise which he did not mention to her, and that the sheikh might raise objections to this transfer, which there might be much trouble in surmounting. Not that Shibley had any right directly to interfere; but the parents of the unfortunate woman were so absolutely dependent upon him, that he had only to command them to refuse to part with their daughter, to be certain of being obeyed. When, therefore, Sheikh Mohanna's son Kassim rode over to see the family, with a view of secretly conducting the negotiations

without Shibley's knowledge, he was im-
mensely relieved at finding that the sheikh
was absent at Damascus; and as the invitation
was both flattering in the highest degree and
financially advantageous—for the mother and
her children were dependent on the pittance
which Shibley chose to allow them — they
hastily and thankfully accepted it, with the
joyful consent of the old people, and the same
afternoon Kassim returned triumphantly to
the paternal mansion with his charges. Here
they were most affectionately and tenderly
received by Amina, in spite of the hot indignation of her mother, who, however, stood in
too great awe both of her brother and her
daughter to give vent to it in the violent
language which was at the tip of her tongue.
Her suppressed emotions were mild, however,
in comparison to those which almost overpowered Sheikh Shibley, when on his return
home he discovered what had occurred. He
stormed at the elders of the village, and
especially at the family of his late wife, threat-
ening them with starvation and other calami-
ties as the consequences of his wrath ; threats,
however, which produced comparatively little

effect, for Kassim had assured them, on the part of Sheikh Mohanna, of protection and pecuniary assistance should they stand in need thereof.

Meantime Sheikh Shibley, still under the influence of his passion, rode on to Teraya, determined to assert his right to keep his children and their mother in his own village, and to expostulate with Sheikh Mohanna on their abduction from it without his consent. He had cooled somewhat before he entered the presence of the old man, and made a mighty effort to retain his self-control; but Sheikh Mohanna, with his quick perception, was in no way deceived by this surface calm, nor by the methodical manner in which his visitor went through the prescribed routine of compliments.

" It grieves me, O sheikh," the latter said, after he had exhausted the list, " to think that this must be the last visit I can pay to you —that practically you have closed the doors to me of that hospitable mansion which from my boyhood I have been accustomed to regard as a second home."

" Not so, my son. I shall always be glad to see you."

" You know that it is not permitted to me
to visit freely in a house which has become the
home of my divorced wife, where at every turn
I run the risk of meeting her."

" I already told you that I disapproved of
your conduct in this matter, more especially
when you informed me of the motives by
which you were actuated. I therefore the
more readily acceded to Amina's request, that
I should invite Fadda and the children here,
because it would aid you in the good resolu-
tion of giving up the idea of marrying your
cousin, if you are prevented from even seeing
her, as you must be, so long as she keeps
Fadda by her side."

Shibley gnashed his teeth at this honest
avowal by Sheikh Mohanna, that his motive
in affording a home to the discarded wife, was
that she might be used as a shield to protect
his niece from the advances of her cousin.

" You have no right," he exclaimed, " thus
to expose me to open insult ! The probability
of my marriage with Amina is a matter of
current rumour. Sada has spoken of it every-
where, and even given it as the reason of my
divorce. That the woman whom it is known

that I desire to marry, should take my divorced wife and children into her own apartments in your house, is an outrage I will not tamely tolerate. I wish to have my children under my own eye in my own village, in charge of their grandparents, their natural protectors, and not subjected to the daily influence of an unbeliever in our religion. It is a matter I shall refer to a council."

"Do as it seems best to you; but remember that the eldest is not yet six, and you cannot claim him till he is seven."

"We shall see about that when the exceptional position of affairs is explained!" said Shibley in a loud tone, rising angrily. "Meantime, beware," he added, with a menacing gesture, "how you add to the suspicions which already exist as to your orthodoxy and devotion to the interests of our nation and our religion. Do not suppose, because men uniformly treat you with respect, that you have no enemies."

Thus saying, Sheikh Shibley strode fiercely from the room, without even the customary politeness of a parting salutation.

He went straight to the house of the Kha-

teeb. " Go," he said to Afifi, who was its only
occupant at the moment, and who, though still
looking pale and weak, was able to be about,
and received him with a beaming smile—" go,
my child, to Sada, the sister of Sheikh Mohanna, and tell her I desire to see her. The
effort will not be too much for you, will it ?
I have been sorry indeed to hear that you
were ill. Do not," he added, " tell any one
but Sada that I am here."

" Oh, I am rapidly recovering," replied the
girl, " and can easily run on your errand."

Afifi knew well why Shibley could not do it
himself, and as she sped on her way, indulged
in a little quiet chuckle, for which, under the
circumstances, she was to be excused. In a
few minutes she returned with Sada; and
though she longed to linger and hear their
conversation, she discreetly retired.

" Sada," said Shibley, after a pause, " the
outrage which I am enduring from your
daughter and Sheikh Mohanna is more than
I can bear."

" I have said so to Amina," replied Sada.
" I have warned her against the consequences
of her conduct."

" And what said she ? "

" That she was doing her duty, and that God would protect her in it."

" Anything more ? "

" Yes; that though she never could have loved you, she might have esteemed you,— henceforth she could never do even that."

Shibley's brow grew as black as night, and his fingers twitched nervously with the violence of his emotion.

" I would save your daughter," he said at last,—" save her to her people, save her to her religion ; but her unruly spirit must first be crushed. So long as she feels wealthy she will defy us ; and she is wealthy, is she not ? "

" She is."

" In what does her wealth consist ? "

" In some valuable jewels which she carried away with her on the night we fled from the Masollams."

" By what right did she take them ? "

" Girius Bey said they belonged to him, and made her take them. He has now given them to her as a present."

" And she has got them with her here ? "

"They are in Mohanna's box, where he keeps all his *koshans*." [1]

"Could you get them for me? You see, if I can get hold of them first, then, if she becomes my wife, she still remains in possession of them?"

"I would not dare. Besides, if Sheikh Mohanna discovered you had stolen them, he would not give you Amina, in order that she might follow the jewels. On the contrary, he would make you restore them."

"But I do not mean him to suspect who has them. However, if you will tell me where the key of the box is, I will get them in some other way."

Sada pondered for some time.

"I do not see," she said at length, "how the possession of the jewels will help you. Amina will never consent to marry you because she has lost her jewels."

"No; but I am going to carry her off by force, and if I do not get the jewels first, I shall never get them afterwards. She will tell Sheikh Mohanna to give them back to Girius Bey."

[1] Title-deeds.

"That is true," said the old woman. "Well, I will tell you where the jewels are; but I must give you this warning, that if you succeed in getting them, and fail in carrying off Amina, then, rather than that she should lose them finally, I will tell who has got them."

"Rest satisfied; I shall not fail, or if I do, I shall restore the jewels. I am no common thief."

"I know that," said Sada, with a glance full of affectionate admiration. "Well, then, the key is kept on the little shelf in the corner of the wall, just above where my brother sleeps, hidden behind some of the sacred books."

"I know the shelf. Where is the box?"

"The box is under the raised divan—exactly at the opposite corner."

"Good. O Sada, not a word of our having met here. It was fortunate that the Khateeb was out. Do not let Afifi gabble; and believe me that I love your daughter too much for any harm to come either to herself or her property. I would save her from the Franji. We shall both lose her again otherwise."

As Shibley rode home, revolving the posi-

tion of matters in his mind, he had formed
two new resolutions, neither of which was
creditable to his moral sense; but then his
moral sense was a very abstract quantity, and
his passions, so to speak, a very concrete one.
Like many others of the human family, his
conduct depended largely upon the amount of
pressure to which he was exposed by temptation, and temptations were crowding upon
him. Since he had felt himself so violently
wronged by Sheikh Mohanna, it had gradually
dawned upon him that the easiest way of
revenging himself for the insult to which he
had been exposed, would be to precipitate the
end of the old man. With Sheikh Mohanna
dead, he would be in fact, as he was now in
name, the head of the family of Zedaan. He
became the natural guardian of Amina and her
mother. His right to marry the former would
be unquestioned, and it was a fate she could
only escape by flight. In whichever direction
he turned now, it was Sheikh Mohanna who
stood in his way. The more he reflected, the
more he perceived that it was absolutely
necessary that Sheikh Mohanna should be got
rid of. Having made up his mind to murder,

there was no great difficulty in reconciling himself to robbery. On thinking over the contract he had made with Madame Masollam, he was more and more struck with its weakness and absurdity. If Amina was satisfied that she was the rightful owner of these precious gems, why should he allow strangers to take possession of them under a vague and unproved claim? When he first heard of their existence, he was glad to appear to come to any terms, just to know accurately all the circumstances of the case; but since his conversation with Sada, who evidently considered the diamonds her daughter's property, he began to take the same view. By the time he entered the gates of Damascus, he had matured a very elaborate and ingenious scheme—provided he could induce the Masollams to fall into it—by which he hoped, in the simplest manner possible, to terminate the existence of Sheikh Mohanna, without incurring any suspicion himself, and, at the same time, to enter into full and comparatively peaceable possession both of Amina and her diamonds. As for any consequences which might possibly result to himself from the utter betrayal of the Masollams

which his plan involved, he had too great a
contempt for their power of mischief to trouble
himself about them. If worse came to worst,
he could always fly with Amina and her treasure to the Jebel Druze, where he would be
safe from pursuit. Indeed, that fertile and
semi-independent region offered so many advantages, political and financial, over the
district he was now inhabiting, that he was
seriously considering the desirability of emi-
grating thither.with his whole village, should
he succeed in his designs, whether he was
troubled afterwards by the Masollams or not.
Nevertheless he was careful to bring the
duplicate copy of the contract for Masollam's
signature, so as to confirm Madame Masollam
in the conviction that he had no intention of
departing from it, unless by common agreement.

While these stormy events had been transpiring at Teraya, the moral atmosphere in
Masollam's house at Damascus had not been
altogether undisturbed. The "Master" had
resented keenly his exclusion from the interview which had taken place between Tigranuhe
and Sheikh Shibley. It was an indignity to

which she had never before dared to subject
him; and his first impulse when Carabet came,
not to invite his co-operation, as he expected,
but to inform him that his sister wished to remain alone with her visitor, was flatly to dis-
obey, and he even rose to do so, when Carabet,
who was a peace-loving man, and foresaw
the storm to which this would give rise,
succeeded in calming his indignation for the
moment. It was roused again, however, when
he heard from Tigranuhe's own lips the nature
of the bargain she had made with Sheikh
Shibley. He had in his infatuation never
given up the idea of making his peace with
Amina and inducing her to return to him.
And he saw in the marriage with the Druse
sheikh, which his wife was plotting to effect,
that she intended to render this impossible.
It was evident to him now why she did not
desire his presence in the room while these
negotiations were being conducted, and he
determined, while appearing to acquiesce in
them completely, to take the first opportunity
he could secretly to thwart them. He therefore suppressed his feelings, and although
Tigranuhe instinctively felt the opposition to

which he gave no utterance, she did not expect it would take an active form. In fact
she rather congratulated herself upon this new
evidence of his subjection. When, therefore,
Shibley presented the contract for Masollam's
signature, the latter read it over with unruffled composure, and with as little intention
of adhering to its terms as Shibley himself.

"I regretted when you were here last," he
said, "that I missed seeing you, both for the
pleasure it would have given me to make your
acquaintance, and also because I always like
to be present myself at delicate negotiations
of this nature. Fortunately I am blessed
with a wife to whom I can absolutely intrust
them. She has narrated to me all the circumstances of your interview, and I thoroughly
agree with the arrangement as it stands."

Masollam managed to pump some youthful
vigour into this speech, and favoured Shibley
with a glance that was meant to be pene-
trating, but which died out harmlessly into
vacancy.

"I have some hesitation in asking you to
sign this now," said the sheikh; "because
since my visit to Teraya I see how easily all

our ends may be gained in another way. I know exactly where the jewels are and how they may be obtained, and I have formed a plan which, if you agree to it, will enable you to take the diamonds with your own hands out of the box in which they are kept. There is one new preliminary condition which is absolutely necessary to the success of my scheme, as you will see yourself, if you will listen while I unfold it to you."

Shibley then told them of the outrage to which he was subjected by the residence of his divorced wife and her children under Amina's charge, and of the insuperable obstacle to his hopes which the protection and authority of Sheikh Mohanna afforded Amina.

" So long as that old man lives," he continued, " I am convinced that neither you, O lady, with all your skill in love-potions, nor I, with all the resources at my command, and I have many, will succeed in abstracting Amina from his control. Now, although I am quite ready to sign this document if you wish it, I should prefer to tear it up, if you will agree to something that cannot be written, and in consideration thereof, I will waive

all demand for pecuniary compensation for
enabling you to recover your gems.   Remembering what you have told me of your knowledge of the properties of herbs, I will leave
you to guess my meaning."

"I think I understand it," said Tigranuhe,
bluntly; "you want me to poison Sheikh Mohanna."

"Not so; I wish you to supply me with the
necessary decoction, and instruct me as to its
use."

"Before I can entertain this new demand, I
must hear your plan in full."

"My plan is this, that we all of us leave
Damascus to-morrow;   that on the following
day I proceed straight to Teraya, while you
move to Hasbaya, or any other place large
enough for your arrival not to cause remark,
and yet near enough to Teraya to be within
striking distance at short notice.   I will at
once call again on Sheikh Mohanna, to express
the greatest contrition for my unseemly conduct on the occasion of our last meeting.   I
know the art of completely winning over the
old man, who, it must be said to his credit,
never retains an angry feeling against any

one; and I will insist on his paying me a visit of reconciliation, with his two sons, and will entertain them all at a banquet to which I will invite other guests. I desire that when the time comes for him to return home, should he refuse to stay and pass the night, he shall be taken so violently ill that one of his sons is despatched with all speed for Amina and her mother; the known skill of the former in medicine, which doubtless she owes to you, will account for this summons. Meantime you will have received notice from me that Sheikh Mohanna and his sons are dining with me, and will arrive late at Teraya; you will probably not be warmly received by Sada and her daughter, but they will scarcely dare to turn you out of the house. Such a breach of hospitality they could not venture upon in the presence of the whole village. I will leave to your own ingenuity the task of effecting your reconciliation, in which probably you will be interrupted by the arrival of the hasty summons for Amina and her mother. On their departure you will be left alone in the house with one or two ignorant and helpless women. When they are asleep you will possess yourselves of the diamonds, and before the dawn you will be on your return journey to Damascus. Amina will meanwhile be watching her uncle through his dying struggles, and after he is dead, she will never leave my house again. What say you of this plan ? "

" Excellently conceived. There is only one objection to it, which you could not have foreseen. Amina will know that her uncle has been poisoned ; for she will recognise the symptoms, and probably apply the antidote."

" As for her knowing that her uncle has been poisoned, that I do not care about. No one will believe the ravings of a girl half distracted with grief. That she should be able to apply an antidote is more serious. Cannot you devise a poison that she will not recognise, when both contingencies would be averted."

Tigranuhe meditated deeply. " Yes," she said at length, " I think I know what will do. If you would like it to take effect about an hour after your guest has done dinner, you can administer it with the coffee that follows that meal. The consequences will be very painful to witness, but Amina has never seen them, nor had them described to her. There is an antidote which sometimes succeeds if given in time, but she will never guess what it is."

"Then you both of you agree to it, and I may tear up these," said Shibley, looking at Masollam, and holding up both the papers between his hands.

"If my wife chooses to supply you with drugs, it is no affair of mine what you do with them," replied the old man.

"You may tear them up. I agree to your proposal," said Tigranuhe; "but I shall require time to prepare the potion. If you will return in a couple of hours, I will have it ready, and instruct you as to its use."

"His plan is a clever one," said Madame Masollam, when the Druse had taken his departure; "but he left out the main feature of it, so far as we are concerned."

"Which was that?" asked Masollam.

"Why, he means to send a party of his people to waylay us, as soon as we are well clear of the village in the early morning, with the diamonds in our possession, and to rob us of them."

"I half suspected as much myself," said Masollam.

Tigranuhe looked at him contemptuously. "And when you half suspected it, how did you propose to meet the danger?" she asked.

"I had not finally determined on any plan."

"Well, I have. We have most fortunately in Khalil Abiad a stanch friend and ardent disciple at Hasbaya, where he wields a great influence. We will go and stay with him. We will tell him that we have reason to fear that we may be robbed on our return from Teraya, and we will not leave that place in the early morning after we have got possession of the property, until at least a dozen well-armed and mounted men arrive to escort us away from it."

Masollam bowed his head in acquiescence: he no longer made any effort to pretend that he had a will of his own; but he had an idea that was actively germinating in his mind, and when Shibley came back he took care to be present, and observed his wife narrowly as

she handed the Druse an ordinary homœo-
pathic bottle, filled, not with globules, but
with a pale-blue liquid.   "A cup of coffee,
with the contents of this phial in it, will do all
that you require," she said.   "One of its chief
merits is that its taste is easily disguised."

CHAPTER IX.

A DOMESTIC CRISIS.

THE distance between Damascus and Teraya is a little over fifty miles, and the first night the travellers determined to sleep at Rashaya. The Masollams were not superior in point of endurance to the average Cook's tourist, and their European experiences had induced habits of luxury which did not accord well with the usual conditions of Syrian travel. They took care to provide themselves with all kinds of culinary delicacies; were very particular about their tea and spirit-lamp, and their own pillows and bedding, so that Sheikh Shibley, much to his disgust, found himself riding out of Damascus followed by a larger train than he anticipated, and could scarcely restrain his impatience at having to stop for afternoon tea.

At Rashaya, Masollam had a friend who insisted that the Druse sheikh should also be his
guest, and who entertained the party sumptu-
ously, Madame Masollam being provided with
sleeping accommodation in the women's apartments, while Masollam and Shibley shared a
room together. As going to bed consists in
throwing off an outer garment, lying down
on a mattress on the floor, and pulling up a
coverlet, the operation is not one which occu-
pies much time. In less than a quarter of an
hour after it was completed, Masollam perceived to his satisfaction that his companion
was profoundly wrapped in slumber. He now
took from his pocket a phial exactly resem-
bling that which he had seen the Druse, on receiving it from the hands of his wife, put into
the breast-pocket of the outer garment which
was now lying by his side. This phial was
also filled with a pale-blue liquid. Silently
and cautiously the old man substituted the
one for the other. "If it is necessary for
the accomplishment of this barbarian's wishes
that my old friend Mohanna should die," he
said to himself, "it is equally necessary to the
accomplishment of mine that he lives; I will

save him, therefore, from the tortures of the
damned by lulling him with the dreams of the.
blest." Thus it happened that the sheikh
rode off next morning with an anodyne instead of a poison in his pocket, while Masollam
and his wife, having parted company with him,
went on their way to Hasbaya.

Shibley had not overestimated his powers
of reconciliation. So skilfully did he assume
an air of contrition ; so much overcome did he
appear with the recollection of his unseemly
behaviour; so entirely did he recognise the
folly of any further insistence in his matrimonial designs as regarded his cousin, that
the old sheikh, whose kind heart was always
ready to accept excuses and to believe in
them, was completely deceived ; the more so
when Shibley asked him to use his influence
with the religious elders to obtain for him a
special dispensation whereby he might be permitted to take back Fadda.

"I know," said Shibley, "how strict the
rule is, but this was a word spoken in haste,
under the influence of a momentary passion ;
perhaps, under the circumstances, an exception
might be made in my favour."

"I doubt it, my son; but I will use what influence I have to forward your wishes."

"I will invite the sheikhs to my house to consider the matter, if you will come to meet them there," Shibley suggested.

"Assuredly I will come."

They then proceeded to discuss the composition of the conclave which should be assembled, and it was agreed that on the second evening following, Mohanna and his sons should dine and sleep at Shibley's. On his return home the latter sent word to this effect to the Masollams.

The firing and singing which took place two nights after, indicated that Ain Ghazal, which was the name of Shibley's village, was *en fête*. For the sheikh had determined to do honour to his distinguished guests, and to receive them with more than usual *éclat*. They were kept in ignorance by their host of the subject which was to be submitted for consideration; but this was a matter of no surprise, the first hours on such occasions being always taken up with compliments and feasting, and the real business only being entered on in the silence of the night. What that business was, it was not

Shibley's intention that his guests should ever know; long before the time for its consideration arrived, he expected that Sheikh Mohanna's illness would be the all-absorbing interest.

While the sheikhs were feasting at Ain Ghazal, the Masollams were approaching Teraya, at which place they arrived shortly after sunset. Sada, Amina, and Fadda happened to be all sitting on the terrace, enjoying the delicious air of evening, and gazing over the rapidly darkening landscape, as the party crossed the *meidan*, and drew up at the foot of the stairs.

Since Santalba's departure, the shadow of Masollam had ceased to haunt Amina; for the first time since she had left The Turrets, a sense of repose seemed to soothe her whole being, and she had never been in the enjoyment of it more completely than at the moment it was destined to be so rudely disturbed. She gave a little scream of terror as she looked over the edge of the terrace. It was no longer the shadow, but the reality which was haunting her now, and in her distress she instinctively clutched at her mother's arm. Sada's eyes followed her daughter's scared look; but she exhibited a courage and a presence of mind on the occasion, which was not to have been expected of her, but which may be accounted for by the confidence she derived from the fact that she was in her own house and in her own village.

" Run in, my child," she said ; " leave me to meet them."

Amina had scarcely disappeared across the court, when the Masollams stepped upon it.

Tigranuhe, who, whatever may have been her faults, had very little of the humbug about her, greeted Sada with a somewhat stately formality, while the prospect of once more seeing Amina had so agitated Masollam, that he was trembling visibly, and presented an aspect of imbecility calculated to inspire pity rather than alarm.

" *Tafuddalu*," said Sada ; which was in fact the only thing she could say, without outraging every oriental *convenance*, and ·which may best be translated by the Italian expression *favorisca*.

" We could not pass your village, on our way back to Damascus from Europe, without stopping to explain what I fear you must have considered our strange treatment of you in

England," said Tigranuhe, "and to correct all
the false impressions which have doubtless
been produced in your mind by our bitter
enemy Santalba, who is here known as Girius
Bey."

"It is past now, and I am happy. I have
recovered my daughter; I am back with her
among my own people : it is unnecessary to
try and explain anything," said Sada.

"I do not want to try and explain or
correct anything," interposed Masollam. " I
only want to ask forgiveness; that is the
reason I have ventured to pay you this visit,
hoping that, notwithstanding the wrongs that
you and your daughter have suffered at my
hands, you would still receive us for a night
under your roof."

Tigranuhe's eyes flashed angrily.

" What nonsense are you talking of wrongs
that they have received at our hands!" she
exclaimed. "Did we not cherish Amina for
twenty-five years as our own daughter? were
we not the means of restoring her to her
mother? and did they not repay us by escap-
ing from the shelter of our roof under cover
of the night? I say that there is much to be

explained on both sides, and many misappre-
hensions to be corrected, and that it was as
much for the purpose of telling our friends
that we have forgiven their ingratitude, which
I know was not intentional, as of excusing
ourselves for an apparent harshness towards
Sada, which we could easily convince her was
not intentional either."

"Let us not go back upon the past," returned Sada. "Both Amina and I are trying
to forget it, and what is forgotten is forgiven.
But you must be fatigued after your journey.
Come in and rest." And she led the way across
the court to the guest-chamber, followed by
the Masollams. Shortly after, Zarifa brought
in some sweetmeats and lemonade; she had
been sent by Amina to report, and Tigranuhe
favoured her with a glance which spoke
volumes of wrath, while she coldly returned
her respectful salutation. Then followed
coffee; and after a little constrained conversation, during which Sada answered Masollam's
inquiries after Mohanna, and expressed her
regret that the sheikh should happen to be
absent, she excused herself on the ground of
domestic duties incidental to the unexpected

arrival of her guests, and sped off to Amina's
room.

"There is nothing to be afraid of," she
said, in reply to her daughter's look of eager
inquiry; "they both seem to me rather sub-
dued. Madame, disagreeable as she always is,
not in the least changed; but the old man
changed altogether. He seems to have grown
twenty years older and to be almost silly."

"You do not know him as I do: he can be
twenty younger again when you least expect
it, and his silliness is only assumed."

"I do not think so; but come and judge
for yourself."

"No; I never wish to see him again," said
Amina, with a slight shudder.

"He has been asking most kindly after you.
I really think he has a sincere regard for you."

"I thought so too once. I am sure I had for
him. That is what makes the idea of seeing
him so painful. It will recall too much."

"Well, please yourself. I must go and see
that some dinner is sent to them. I have
done all that civility requires, and shall leave
them to eat it by themselves."

This arrangement suited Tigranuhe very

well, who was thinking more about those
diamonds, from all allusion to which she had
so carefully abstained, than about her hosts;
but it was far otherwise with Masollam, whose
morbid craving to see Amina·was becoming
almost intolerable to him. The sensational
rapport which existed between the "Master"
and his wife, now that they no longer had
any sentiment in common, produced a friction
which positively amounted to physical pain.
As there are certain sounds, the mere thought
of which will set one's teeth on edge, so other
distressing sensations can be produced by
causes which originate in those hypersensitive
regions of our being, which are affected by the
moral conditions of those with whom we are in
contact. Masollam was acutely conscious of
every change in his wife's mood, even though
it found no expression in utterance; and she
could have told him every time he was thinking of Amina by a certain sense of constriction
in the chest, which latterly Amina's own presence had always given rise to. Each time
that by an act of intense longing Masollam
drew as it were the influence of her he loved
into himself, Tigranuhe could recognise it by

this pain, and it made her furious. It was while they were thus sitting together over the repast that Sada had provided for them, vainly attempting to do it justice, that they each arrived at the same mental conclusion, and that they both knew that they had arrived at it. They perceived that life together involved an amount of suffering which had become intolerable, but that life apart was impracticable; their interests were too complicated, and involved those of too many others, to make it possible to divide them either morally or materially. Those interests must remain centred, if not in both of them, at least in one of them; and to that end one must be got rid of; and the question naturally suggested itself to each, Which? It was a question which neither of them had the least difficulty in deciding. As the answer occurred to them at precisely the same moment, and involved such fatal consequences, they both, in obedience to the same impulse, looked up, and each recognised the dread import of the other's glance. Had they spoken all their thoughts, they would not have known more accurately what had passed through the mind

of each ; hence it will appear that, under the
new and highly sensitive conditions which are
now overtaking the race, people who are anti-
pathetic to each other will find it more difficult than they did formerly to live together in
intimate relations.

The Masollams were by no means similarly
affected by the painful revelation they had
severally received.

Now that the suspicion he had long entertained, that Tigranuhe would take his life, had
ripened into certainty, the Master was seized
with a fit of abject terror : a cold perspiration bedewed his forehead, his teeth began
to chatter, and he staggered to his feet and
tottered out into the courtyard, not to conceal his panic, for that, he knew, was impossible, but to draw a breath of fresh air.
Tigranuhe followed his retreating figure with
a scornful glance. Though she knew that he
had made up his mind to murder her if he
could, she did not quail, but rather contem-
plated the situation as an expert American
duellist might, who was on " shooting at sight
terms " with his opponent, if he knew that
the latter had never handled a rifle or a pistol

in his life. It was rather a relief to feel
forced, in self-defence, to decide upon an act for
which she had for some time past desired an
excuse for perpetrating : and Tigranuhe was
not without her own moral standard ; indeed,
at one time it had been of the highest, and
now, if her nature could throw the darkest
shadows, it was because it had in it the capac-
ity for casting the highest lights. Hitherto
she sought in vain for some justification for
the impulse which moved her to take her
husband's life, and, unable to find one, had
heroically struggled against it. She felt the
more strongly impressed to resist this tendency, as there were moments when she was
conscious of a general homicidal propensity,
especially while dabbling with her poisons;
and she knew that it was a temptation which,
if it were not resisted with the utmost force
of her will at the outset, might lead her, as
it has already so many who have figured
in the annals of history and of crime, to
extremities which she could not afterwards
justify to her conscience, and which she would
consequently have reason to regret. She had
therefore refused even to entertain the idea

of poisoning her husband, although it had repeatedly occurred to her as the simple solution of the difficulties created by his protracted existence, and although she felt convinced that he was deliberately and wilfully resisting the will of God in continuing to live, more especially since he had sacrificed his gifts to an unholy passion. For, strange as it may seem to those who have never met such characters, and who may possibly doubt that they exist, Tigranuhe was firmly and honestly convinced that she was a priestess by divine right—the prophetess of the new age—especially chosen by God to establish the supremacy, and to inaugurate the reign of woman. She had used man, in the form of Masollam, as the ladder by which to mount to her present lofty elevation; she had gradually, by an almost unconscious process of absorption for years past, been appropriating his knowledges and acquiring his gifts; until now she could not only afford to do without him, but his presence had become a positive hindrance and embarrassment,—unless, indeed, he chose humbly to accept the position, subordinate to herself, for which he had been de-

signed by a merciful and all-wise Providence.
From the day when these personal ambitions
—which in her mind assumed the form of
divine inspirations — took possession of her
being, there commenced within her a secret,
and at first totally unconscious, antagonism to
Masollam. They were working on different
lines, but their divergence was so latent, that
it only slowly developed under the pressure
of circumstances ; and this pressure was only
accentuated when the influence of Santalba
was introduced still further to complicate
matters.

Before the discovery of Sada by Masollam,
he too had been tempted from the path of duty
and of strict service by the blind devotion of
his disciples, and the wealth with which that
devotion had supplied him. The demons of
pride and avarice had effected a subtle entrance,
and at first almost imperceptibly tainting his
motives, had gradually acquired a mastery over
them—still speciously, however, deluding him
with the belief that, in obeying their promptings, he was acting in accordance with those
higher intuitions, under the plausible guise of
which they inspired his soul. These became

more delusive in the degree in which they assumed the form of vision or supernatural impression.

Santalba, on the other hand, who, while developing his inner consciousness, and sensitising his whole being to its promptings, had not allowed his individuality to fall under a control he could not cognise, remained true to his highest inspirations; and it was under these new relative conditions that these three people, whose intercourse for some years previously had been but slenderly maintained, had found themselves once more compelled to act together. For when Masollam discovered the existence of Sada, he at once wrote to Santalba announcing a fact in which he, as the saviour of Amina, was so nearly interested. The correspondence which followed led to the visit of Sada and the Masollams to England; and Santalba, ignorant of the changes which had been operating in the Masollams, believed that in undertaking that visit they were both actuated by motives as pure as were his own. But, as we have seen, the motives of the Masollams were not only morally tainted, but, being personal, they were of necessity mutu-

ally antagonistic; and hence, when they all
three met at The Turrets to work together,
they immediately came into a collision, the
nature and results of which form the subject
of our story. Masollam's object was to get
possession of Sebastian Hartwright's money
with the aid of Santalba, in the prosecution of
an elaborately devised plan, the full scope of
which will become more apparent later, but
which Santalba foiled.   Tigranuhe's object
was not merely to secure possession of this
money, but to obtain an ascendancy over Santalba.   For this reason she remained behind
with him in Paris, in the hope, afterwards,
with his assistance, to subjugate Amina more
completely to her will than she could do while
the girl gave her entire devotion to Masollam;
and, with these two as her allies, to achieve
her final conquest of the Master.   When she
had once gained the recognition from them
all of her feminine spiritual headship, she
intended to inaugurate in the West the
great movement by which the human race
was to be regenerated through woman.   She
would remain the mysterious veiled prophetess, visible only to the most deeply in-

itiated, and rarely even to them. This was necessary, as she could not speak any European language well enough to converse fluently; and even if it had been otherwise, she shrank from meeting in conversation the acute, logical, and highly instructed intellect of the West. They could be met by the Master, who, in recognition of this new avatar, was to sink to the position and assume the title of "the Consort"; by Santalba, "the Knight"; by Sebastian, "the Squire"; by Carabet, "the lackey"; and lastly, by Amina, the "Vestal," who was to give lectures, take the chair at evening meetings, and preside at those *réunions* to which all fashionable London was to be invited in the magnificent mansion which was to be taken as their residence with Sebastian's money. It is scarcely necessary to say that the title which Tigranuhe had reserved for herself was that of Queen.

From a purely social point of view, it is to be regretted that this splendid projection of an oriental imagination should have had from the first to struggle against difficulties beneath which it utterly collapsed in embryo. The opening of a sort of palace in Mayfair, where

a mysterious queen, invisible to the common
herd, should hold a court from which regal
hospitalities, spiced with mysticism, were dis-
pensed by a lovely virgin, aided by such
adepts as Masollam, Santalba, Sebastian, and
Carabet, and which should not only represent
the supremacy of woman generally, but accord
her those rights which she demands in vain in
other quarters, would have been the sensation
of the season. And considering the present
mood of the great metropolis, it is very
probable that Queen Tigranuhe would have
received the spiritual allegiance of thousands.
All this was ruined by the infatuation which
induced Masollam to fall in love with Amina,
and by the refusal of Santalba, from the moment when she first met him in Paris, to
recognise in her any of that supreme spiritual
authority which she endeavoured to assume.
She had not been so unsuccessful in the East :
here in Damascus she had made many disciples among women,—having been engaged
in an active propaganda in harems, the entry
to which was prohibited to Masollam,—and in
this queen of oriental cities she now determined to erect her throne. As a spiritual

one, it must needs be invisible. Indeed she well knew that the Government would not permit any other; but it would be reared in the hearts of women, and, as its influence spread, it would render every harem a hell upon earth to its unhappy lord. The collapse of that religion which had degraded the position of the sex more than any other, must inevitably follow a general feminine revolt; and it would be a divine Nemesis indeed if the phœnix which arose from its ashes was the apotheosis of woman. From which it will be seen that Tigranuhe was a persevering person, not easily baffled; and that with the instinct of true genius, when defeated in one quarter, she could, with the utmost rapidity of conception, transfer her field of operations, and map out her plan of campaign in another. But to succeed in it the Master could not be allowed even the position of consort. Emancipated women of the East, who have suffered so long at the hands of the other sex, would never permit men the dignity of this rank. He would be expected to accept the service and the name of " the Slave." As Tigranuhe looked out of the door and saw Masollam sit-

ting on the edge of the fountain in the court,
and felt that she had excited those sentiments
of fear and rage and vengeance which were
convulsing his nature, she perceived that there
was no longer room for doubt or hesitation.
He was the one great obstacle to the successful accomplishment of the divine work
on earth which was to be achieved through
woman. This was no ordinary homicidal
temptation of the kind she had already resisted : it was a divine impulse, mixed, it
might be, with an instinct of self-preservation ; but was not her life the first essential
to the great mission with which she was
intrusted ?

"Poor old man !" she said to herself reflec-
tively, as she mixed some sour milk with her
rice and stewed lamb, " I will manage it so
that he shall go to sleep quietly, and wake in
a region where he can be of more use to me.
God knows I bear him no malice because he
has made my life a torture for months past.
He has been overpowered by a class of temptations which he had not strength to resist."

She had never thought so kindly of him as
when she knew he was plotting her murder,

and had decided on anticipating his designs by removing him on the first opportunity from this sublunary sphere—had never felt so entirely at peace with herself, or so conscious of the singleness and integrity of her motives.

" Master," she called out in a more conciliatory and gentler tone than she had used towards him for months past, " the sun has given me a little headache during our ride this afternoon.   Won't you come in and make me a little tea ? "

CHAPTER X.

THE TRAGEDY.

THE Master started as if he had been shot
when he heard this unexpected summons, so
extreme was the nervous tension from which
he was suffering at the moment. His first
impression was that it concealed a trap of
some kind, and he hesitated a moment before
he could pluck up courage to obey it. He was
aware that Tigranuhe, prior to her departure
on this enterprise—the main feature of which
was not unattended with peril—had armed
herself with a pretty little silver‑mounted
revolver, and an exquisite dagger of minute
dimensions, the blade of which, of damascene
workmanship, left nothing to be desired, and
would have commanded a high price at Abou
Anticha's, or at all events—which comes nearly

to the same thing—that eminent curiosity-
dealer would have demanded a high price
for it from the ingenuous tourist; but he reflected that to assassinate him then and there
would be to defeat her own ends, and that for
the moment, at all events, he was safe. With
drooping head, and an air of extreme submission, therefore, he obeyed the call. He had
scarcely done so, and was engaged in unpack-
ing the saddle-bags which contained the spirit-
lamp, when Sada entered. As he did not feel
that it would be polite to begin boiling water
in her presence, and as, moreover, he was extremely anxious to recur to the topic of Amina,
and discover whether it might not be possible
to procure an audience with her, he suspended
his operations; while Sada, who had yielded to
an impulse, partly of curiosity, partly of politeness, and partly of gossip in returning to her
guests, inquired of them as to the incidents of
their journey from Europe, and expatiated on
her own travelling fortunes and misfortunes,
speedily becoming as communicative and confidential as though nothing had ever happened
to sow the seeds of distrust between them.
Thus, without being obliged to ask any ques-

tions directly, Masollam heard a great deal about Amina, and although Sada could tell them nothing that she had not heard already from Shibley, Tigranuhe was glad to let her gabble on. She interrupted her once to inquire about the Sebastian Hartwrights and Reginald Clareville. Sada said she had been present at the wedding, immediately after which the young couple had disappeared, she knew not whither; while Reginald had travelled with them as far as Paris, in which city they had finally parted from him when he accompanied them to the train to see them off on their journey to the East. Since then she had heard nothing of them, though she knew that from time to time Amina had received letters, in regard to the contents of which she was extremely reserved. In her turn Sada asked, not without kindness, after Carabet, by whom, she remarked, she had been treated with a respect and attention she should never forget, albeit she was not permitted to leave her own rooms; and she observed laughingly that he had incidentally taught her a trade, which would always keep her from want. She had actually manufactured an antique since her return to

Teraya, which she had sent to Damascus by Shibley, and which he had disposed of there to the waiter of a hotel for five hundred piastres, although its manufacture had cost her nothing, and been the amusement of a couple of hours.

"Don't you think," said Tigranuhe at last, still disposed to be amiable to "the Master," now that he had so few hours, or at most days, to live, "that you could induce Amina just to come here for one moment before we retire to rest? it has now become so late that we must all go to bed soon. We propose starting before you are up to-morrow morning, and I know that my dear husband would like to see Amina once more, if only, as he says, to ask her forgiveness before he—dies," she added calmly.

Masollam felt a cold shiver run down his back; but he gave a ghastly smile, for the prospect of seeing Amina rallied him.

"Tell her it is my last prayer," he said.

"Who talks of dying?" ejaculated Sada; "have you any serious illness? You certainly do not look well."

"Tell your daughter I have a mortal disease

on me, and if I do not see her now, I shall
never see her again in this world."

"Poor old creature!" mused Tigranuhe;
"he sees he cannot fight against me, and has
reconciled himself to his fate; I shall certainly
make it as easy for him as possible."

"May God have pity on you, and restore
you to health; I shall certainly go at once,
and make her come," said Sada—who was a
kind-hearted soul, though a goose—and went
off on her mission. In a few moments she
returned with Amina, looking very pale, very
statuesque, and, in her native costume, very
beautiful. As she turned her full unfaltering
gaze, first on one and then on the other of the
visitors, Masollam was unable to restrain his
emotion and buried his face in his hands; even
Tigranuhe shrank from meeting her eye, and
lowered her own lids, furious with herself as
she reflected that she, the queen of the sex,
should be compelled to this act of tacit submission to a subject. She determined at once
to repair the error and assert her dignity.

"I am surprised, Amina, at your conduct,"
she said, in a severe tone. "Although we, your
oldest friends, whom you have been accus-

tomed to consider your own parents, who have never treated you with anything but love and kindness, to whom you owe everything, have been in the house for several hours, you decline to see us, although we have come out of our way expressly to visit you, and only at last obey with reluctance the summons of a dying man."

This speech jarred so much on Masollam from its first word to its last, which was especially repugnant to him, that before Amina could answer he interposed—

"It is true that Tigranuhe considers me a dying man; and although I am not conscious myself of being in so serious a condition as she declares, her intuition, as you know, in cases of disease is so infallible, that I am willing to accept as correct her statement that I have only a short time to live—a few days, I think you said, my dear," and he turned to Madame, who bowed her head in assent. "You see," he pursued with a smile, in the apparent resignation of which Amina thought she detected the gleam of another meaning,—"you see she will only grant me a few days more of earthly existence; and as

all men in the immediate presence of death
desire, or should desire, to make reparation
for wrongs they may have committed, and
should seek reconciliation with, and forgiveness from, those whom they are conscious of
having injured, my predominant feeling, ever
since Tigranuhe told me that I had not much
longer to live, has been to see you. Do not
think, my darling daughter, that I concur in
her reproaches. On the contrary, I consider
your consenting to meet us not only an act
of condescension"—and as Madame's eyes
flashed daggers on him, he added, as though
purposely to infuriate her still more—" towards us both, which we in no way deserve,
but of especial compassion and charity towards
myself. In Madame Masollam's name and my
own, I thank you for it."

The old man drew himself up with an air
of dignity, and Amina's quick perceptions
instantly sensed the storm that was raging
between those with whom her own relations
had once been so intimate, and she was literally appalled by its fury. Like an electrician,
whose calculations are all thrown out by the violence of an unexpected atmospheric disturbance,

she looked in blank dismay from one to the other;
and as the vague dread of some unknown catastrophe crept over her, all feeling of fear for
herself, which had been the predominant sentiment when she entered the room, gave place
to one of compassion for the strange couple in
whose presence she was. It was they who
were in danger, not she, and it was their
salvation from each other, and not her own
from them, that was to be achieved. A great
love seemed to surge into her being—a love
which, by reason of the peace that it contained, might still these raging waters.

"You are right, my mother," she said,
taking Tigranuhe's hand and kissing it, " and
my father is wrong. It is I who have to ask
forgiveness—not you, nor he. Perhaps if I
had acted differently, I could have prevented
much that has happened. I thank God that
He has brought you both under my roof, and
given me an opportunity of telling you this,
and of assuring you of a love that is still
ready, at the cost of any sacrifice, to serve
you both ; for," she added, in a low sweet tone,
" I perceive that, since I have left you, both
stand sorely in need of love and service."

Masollam groaned; he too felt that a
change was being worked within him, and
that the passion of which he had been the
slave, was giving place to a nobler sentiment.
In a softened mood he stole a look at Tigranuhe, in the hope that he might perceive
in her an indication of yielding to Amina's tender influence; but what had melted him had
petrified her. She had instinctively felt that
to allow that sacred fire to touch her icy heart,
was to abdicate her throne for ever. The
authority of a divine love spoke through that
gentle girl, and to obey it was to acknowledge
Amina's supremacy as queen by right of that
love. At no moment of her life had her
hatred of her adopted daughter been more
intense. Amina felt it, and cast a despairing
glance at Masollam; their eyes met for a
moment, but she read in those of the old
man the evidence of her triumph. If she
had failed with Tigranuhe, she had won with
him.

"I do not think," she said, affectionately
placing her hand in his, "that my presence
here just now can be of any more use. May
God protect you both to-night; and be sure,

however early you may start in the morning, I will see you before you leave."

Amina glided from the room, followed by Sada, and the Masollams were alone.

"I was a fool," said Tigranuhe, "to send for the girl; but I yielded weakly to what I felt to be an overpowering desire on your part."

"Thank you," replied Masollam, meekly; "you did me a service I shall never regret."

"But I shall," muttered Madame; and then she added in a sharp tone, "it is strange that the summons has not yet arrived for Amina from Shibley. It is near midnight. It should have been here an hour or more ago. I was in hopes it would arrive while the girl was in the room with us; in fact, that was an additional reason for my sending for her."

"I have something to say," said Masollam, "to which I fear you will only listen with impatience." He spoke timidly, and with great hesitation.

"Then don't say it."

"I must; a great deal depends upon your answer."

"Go on, then," said Tigranuhe, with a contemptuous shrug of her shoulders.

"I want to know whether you will not abandon the idea of depriving Amina of her diamonds. We do not need them. We are abundantly rich."

"You might well say that I would only listen to such rubbish with impatience," flashed out Tigranuhe. "Her diamonds, indeed! Since when have you come to consider them hers? Abundantly rich! We can never be abundantly rich as long as there is more wealth to be had. If a great deal depends upon my answer—No! there you have it. Now I am going out on a reconnoitring expedition."

"Won't you have your tea first?"

"No; you can be getting it ready. I must wait another hour to give them all time to get to sleep; but I am impatient to take a general survey. Fortunately there is a good moon;" and Tigranuhe stepped out into the court.

Masollam got the tea, lighted the spirit-lamp, poured one cupful of water into the pot, which he then put upon the lamp, took the phial out of his pocket, which he had abstracted from

Shibley's, waited until the water boiled, keeping an eye upon the courtyard all the time; and when it had boiled, he poured the whole contents of the phial into it, adding the necessary tea. He then took another cup, poured a few drops of the tea, after it had sufficiently drawn, into it, and watched steadily. As he observed Tigranuhe approaching, he lifted this cup to his lips, and continued apparently to sip it, as she took her seat on the cushions near him.

"You like your tea stronger than I do, to-night especially, when you will have to keep awake, so I poured out mine and drank it, without waiting for you. I am afraid yours may have got a little cold." And he set down his almost empty cup, from which in fact he had drunk nothing, and poured out another for his wife.

"It will be a very easy matter," she said, taking the cup mechanically. "The house is already so quiet, that I can go to work with safety in an hour. How thirsty that salt pickle they gave us at dinner has made me!" and she drank the whole cup at a draught. "How frightfully strong you have made it!

and it has been standing so long it has got
quite bitter. Give me a biscuit, and make me
some more, very weak."

Masollam obeyed, and Madame sipped the
second cup deliberately, smoking a nargileh
the while.

"Now," she said, when she had finished it,
and the hour had almost expired, "I shall
go to work seriously, and," she continued as
a sudden suspicion flashed across her mind,
"you must come with me; after what you
said about my refusal to give up the jewels
having important consequences, I can't trust
you; you are quite capable in your blind devotion to that girl to give the alarm, and—look
here," and Madame pulled the little revolver
from her breast, "if I have the slightest suspicion of treachery, you know what to expect,
and that I can be absolutely depended upon
in a matter of this sort. Now, take off your
shoes, and come along."

Shibley's instructions were so exact that
Tigranuhe had no difficulty in following them.
It is true the door of the sheikh's room was
roughly bolted; but Tigranuhe in her preliminary expedition had discovered the trick of

pushing the bolt back with a lever. The room itself was unfurnished, as all Druse rooms are. The key was easily found in the shelf in the corner, and the box under the raised divan.

"Help me to pull it out," said Tigranuhe in a whisper; "it is impossible to find the casket in this confusion of deeds and manuscripts otherwise."

With a combined effort, the pair succeeded in dragging the box from its hiding-place, and Tigranuhe began to rummage among its contents. At last, with an exclamation of satisfaction, she grasped her prize. It was almost immediately followed by a groan, for on raising herself from her stooping position, she was seized with a sudden deadly faintness, accompanied by a violent spasm.

"Ah!" she ejaculated, as, recognising the symptom, the truth flashed upon her; and hastily raising her left hand, which still clasped the pistol, she had just time to discharge it at Masollam, and to hear the sharp cry of pain which followed the report, before she herself sank to the ground, and lost all other consciousness but that of the agony which was convulsing her frame.

Amina was pacing her room in agitated thought, when the sound of the pistol-shot started her from her meditations. She had found it utterly impossible to compose herself to rest after leaving the Masollams, so heavily did the presentiment of an impending misfortune weigh upon her. She seemed to be walking upon a mine which might explode at any moment ; but in what direction its disastrous effects would be chiefly felt, she had not been able clearly to discern. Ever since her uncle had accepted Shibley's invitation, she had been conscious of a vague feeling of uneasiness about him, and this at one time increased to such an extent, that she at last had extracted a promise from him if possible to return the same night. Her anxiety was not allayed by the fact that it was now past midnight, and there were no signs of him. But since her interview with the Masollams, her fears had taken another direction. She knew now that a great danger was under her own roof, and the figure which seemed to cast its dark shadow over her soul was no longer that of the Master, but of Tigranuhe.

Gradually her own heart seemed turning to

stone ; a chill took possession of her frame, and she began physically to experience, especially in her extremities, a sensation of intense cold. There was so little of imagination in this, that she had been obliged to wrap herself up in a warm shawl, and even now as she walked up and down, she found herself stamping her feet in her effort to keep up the circulation. It seemed as though she was becoming slowly petrified into the image and likeness of Tigranuhe . herself. Wild ambitions began to fire her soul. Visions of regal pageants and coronation ceremonies, in which she was always the central figure, rose before her distorted imagination; but there was always one obstacle which, at the critical moment, seemed to interpose between her and the realisation of these lofty aspirations. She perceived that to succeed she must kill Masollam, and then a vague dread seemed to seize her that if she did not kill Masollam, he would certainly kill her. It was at the moment when she was struggling back into a sense of her own identity, and when she was beginning to perceive the drift of the painful revelation which was made to her through its

temporary obscuration by that of Tigranuhe,
—in fact it was at the very moment that a
conviction that the Masollams were in danger
from each other, and that she must rush to
their rescue, was forcing itself upon her—that
the sharp ring of the shot burst upon the
still air of night, and she knew that she
would be just too late. She rushed wild-
ly to the guests' apartments, although the
sound had not seemed to come from that
direction, and found the room lighted but
empty, the deserted tea-apparatus and still
smouldering nargileh showing how recently
the occupants had left it. She flew across
the court, entering her uncle's outer apartment, where the open door of his inner room
revealed the presence of intruders. The moon-
light was streaming into it through a large
uncurtained window, and at the door lay
Masollam, moaning and breathing heavily;
writhing beside her uncle's open strong-box
was stretched Tigranuhe, her frame from time
to time contorted by violent spasms, her
teeth set, her hands clenched, but her gleam-
ing eyes showed that she was fully conscious. At a glance Amina perceived that her

left hand clasped a pistol, and her right her own jewel-box. She stooped down, and gently, but with great difficulty, disengaged both the one and the other. She had scarcely done so when Sada, accompanied by Zarifa, both of whom the report had also aroused, entered the room. Tigranuhe glared at them savagely, like some mortally wounded wild animal, unable to turn upon its pursuers. She evidently struggled to speak; but her jaws were so tightly locked, that for some moments the effort was in vain. At length the spasm relaxed in its fury, and she murmured the name of a potent drug. Amina's quick apprehension at once perceived its full import.

"Leave her for the present," she said to the two women, "and look to Daoud Effendi. I will return in a moment;" and she sped to her own room, returning in a few moments with a lamp, the medicine, and the appliances necessary for administering it. She succeeded in giving Tigranuhe a powerful dose before the recurrence of the next spasm. She now turned to Masollam, who had been raised into a sitting posture, and whom she was relieved to find was more frightened than hurt. The ball had passed through the upper or more fleshy part of the shoulder, grazing the bone, and she set herself to stay the profuse bleeding. This was soon sufficiently stanched to enable him to be removed to a bed which had been prepared for him, for the whole household was now on the alert, and Amina was in a position to give her undivided attention to Tigranuhe. She had her carried to her own room, whither, when she had gone for the medicine, she had already conveyed the diamonds, so that the motive of the attempted crime remained a mystery to all save Amina, Sada, and Zarifa,—and of these three, Sada alone knew its origin and secret history, and in her heart she cursed Shibley. It was not to hand these precious gems back to the Masollams, that she had told him how they might be stolen. But then Sada did not know that at that moment a band of armed Druses were in the act of leaving Ain Ghazal, for the purpose of stealing them back again; still less did those Druses know that a strong party of armed Christians were on their way from Hasbaya to protect the thieves.

Meantime, throughout the whole of that

weary and eventful night, did Amina watch by the side of the bitterest enemy she had in the world, mitigating, by the most skilful and tender ministrations, the agonies of her suffering, and aiding by the magic of her healing touch, and the life that flowed through it, the powerful but less subtle effect of the antidote she was administering.

CHAPTER XI.

SHEIKH SHIBLEY FAILS IN HIS PLOT.

IN inviting some neighbouring sheikhs to meet Sheikh Mohanna at Ain Ghazal, Shibley's motive was, as our readers are aware, quite other than that which he had made the pretext for the assembly when he had discussed the subject with his venerable guest. He desired their presence there for many reasons. He had no fear that any accusations by Amina, even should she venture to make them, of foul play on his part, would be credited. He was known to entertain the profoundest respect and affection for the old sheikh, and it was not likely that he would choose the occasion, when so many witnesses would be present, to murder him, the more especially when, as he would be able to prove

to them, his own interests would be only injured thereby. Amina was scarcely known to
them, and, as a stranger and alien in religion,
was still distrusted; and if, in his desire to save
her uncle's life, he sent for her to exert her
medical skill upon him, he could not afford
better evidence than he was ignorant of the
malady by which his relative had been seized,
or he would have avoided laying himself open
to so grave an accusation as, by his own act, he
thus enabled her to bring against him. On the
other hand, he intended to say that he had
asked her uncle to agree to their union; that
the latter had consented; but that, under the
peculiar circumstances of the case, they had
both considered the subject one which should
be submitted to a council of their spiritual
friends, as Amina's contumacy raised a serious
question; that this had become all the more
important now that she was evidently about
to lose her only protector. He then meant to
explain why he desired their consent to con-
stitute himself that protector; and, provided
her own mother would agree to that arrangement, he would ask them to approve of his
determination to keep them both in his house.

In fact he saw his way to strengthening his
own position by making this grave catastrophe
the occasion of taking these influential neighbours into his confidence in his domestic affairs
and matrimonial designs.   With a view to
preparing their minds in this direction, he
had taken occasion privately to throw out a
hint to one or two of his leading guests as to
the nature of the subject which was to come
under discussion, among others to the Khateeb
of Teraya, who was a man of high authority,
and much looked up to in all matters touching
religion in the neighbouring villages as well
as in his own. Shibley felt that he could
count absolutely upon the devotion of this
man to his interests, for he had ever reckoned
him among his warmest friends, and had more
than once discussed fully and confidentially
with him his projects in regard to Amina, and
the difficulties by which they were surrounded.
He had always met with the warmest sympathy, for the Khateeb was somewhat jealous
of Sheikh Mohanna, and resented the introduction into the village of a strange girl, who
seemed disposed to set at defiance the highest
spiritual authority, and to invoke successfully

in so doing her uncle's powerful protection.
But within the last three or four days other
influences had been at work on the Khateeb's
mind, of which Shibley knew nothing. His
wife was an ambitious scheming woman, who
was well aware of her daughter's affection for
the young and handsome sheikh, and who
was extremely anxious to gratify it, and thus
to form an alliance with the ancient family of
Zedaan ; and she had made Shibley ever a welcome guest in her house, in the hope that her
daughter might inspire him with a passion
which might induce him to divorce his present
wife.

She had never yet ventured to allude to
this delicate subject to her husband. When,
however, she heard him express a somewhat
indignant surprise that Shibley should have
divorced his wife for the sake of Amina,
without first consulting him, she thought the
moment opportune. She explained that their
own daughter was pining away for love of the
young sheikh; that Amina had, on the other
hand, manifested her dislike to him by taking
his divorced wife under her roof to serve as a
protection against him ; that the interests of

the nation would be in no way served by assisting Shibley to marry a girl who hated him, and refused to consider herself a Druse ; whereas the interests, not only of the nation, but of their own family, would be served by the Khateeb becoming Shibley's father-in-law, while it would secure the happiness of the daughter they both loved so fondly. In fact, with so much feminine skill and logic did Afifi's mother ply her arguments, that she ended by completely converting her husband to her way of thinking ; and he went to Ain Ghazal with the secret intention of thwarting Shibley's designs in regard to Amina by every means in his power.

As, according to Tigranuhe's calculation, the poison was not to take effect for an hour after it was administered, Shibley was obliged to exert all his ingenuity when the repast was over to postpone the discussion of his affairs ; but the sheikhs were beginning to wax im-patient, and the Khateeb had just suggested that they should enter upon the business which had called them together, when it was observed that Sheikh Mohanna had fallen into a profound slumber. All efforts, consistent with politeness, to rouse him proved unavailing; and as Shibley felt little doubt that this was the first indication of the action of the poison, to be followed before very long by some more violent symptom, and as he could find no further excuse for delaying the discussion, he determined to enter upon it, the more especially as it would perhaps afford an opportunity of having something decided before the confusion took place which would result from a more violent manifestation of sickness. He therefore said that he regretted that a fit of drowsiness should render Sheikh Mohanna incapable of listening to what he had to say, which was, shortly to lay before them the decision to which he and the sheikh had arrived,—that it would be desirable, both in Amina's interests and in that of the family of Zedaan, that the daughter of the late Sheikh Sâleh should be allied to its present head, and compelled to give in her adhesion to the Druse religion, and should henceforth be identified with the nation, not merely by blood, but by marriage and by faith. He went on to say that he had not only secured the consent of Sheikh Mohanna to this arrangement, but of

Amina's mother Sạda, and, he would venture
to say, of the Khateeb, to whom he referred in
confirmation of this statement. To his surprise, the Khateeb replied in guarded and
qualified terms. He said, that since he had
last expressed a general sympathy with Sheikh
Shibley's wishes, two events had occurred.
One was a conversation with Sheikh Mohanna,
whose language did not by any means accord
with what had just fallen from Sheikh Shibley;
and the other was the divorce by the latter of
his wife, which had taken place without his
knowledge, and, in his opinion, prematurely :
it should have followed rather than preceded
the meeting they were now holding. Under
these circumstances, he suggested that they
had better postpone any further discussion of
the matter until some future day, when Sheikh
Mohanna would be able to take part in it.

Shibley bit his lip with vexation. He began to suspect, as he watched the old sheikh
slumbering peacefully, that Tigranuhe had
played him false. More than two hours had
now elapsed since he had emptied the phial
into the cup of coffee he had himself handed
the old sheikh, and the latter showed no sign

of pain or other disturbance. He suggested to
his guests that the sleep did not seem natural,
and that perhaps Sheikh Mohanna was seriously ill; but they refused to entertain this
idea, being accustomed to sound sleepers, and
those who lived near prepared to take their
departure, among them the Khateeb, while
others proceeded to make themselves comfortable there for the night. Shibley now felt
no doubt that he was betrayed; and he even
feared that the Masollams might effect the
robbery before his own men, who had not
yet started, could overtake them. He had
already given them their orders, and now
went out to hurry them off. As he did so, he
whispered in the ear of their leader that the
woman was not to be allowed to escape alive.
He knew that this involved his own flight to
the Jebel Druze; but he was too thirsty for
vengeance, and too much enraged at the failure
of his scheme so far, to allow this consideration to weigh with him. Moreover, he still
had hopes by a bold dash of being able to
carry off Amina with him. After what he
had said at the meeting, which would certainly be reported to Sheikh Mohanna, the

latter would perceive that he had been invited to Ain Ghazal under false pretences; and although he would remain ignorant of the full blackness of the treachery, from the fatal consequences of which he had so narrowly escaped, Shibley could not expect again to be received by him as a friend.

The day succeeding this tragic night had not dawned, when a messenger arrived at Ain Ghazal, in hot haste from Teraya. Shibley had been too much agitated to sleep. He was revolving in his mind projects of violence, and anxiously awaiting some news of the mission of robbery and vengeance which he had despatched, when he heard a horse clatter into the courtyard. Hurriedly rising, he met a young man, whom he recognised as one of Sheikh Mohanna's retainers.

"Where is the sheikh?" asked the messenger excitedly. "He must return at once to Teraya. Two visitors arrived last night, and they have been trying to murder each other, and are lying at the point of death, and the *sittat*[1] Sada and Amina urgently beg the sheikh to return at once."

[1] Ladies.

"What kind of visitors?" asked Shibley, whose heart began to sink within him at the prospect of losing alike his treasure and his vengeance.

"An old man and an old woman; they looked like Nusrani."[1]

"Did they come alone?"

"Two baggage-animals and a *muchareh*."[2]

"Come in. I will see whether it is possible to wake the sheikh; he has not been well."

Sheikh Mohanna had slept off the first effects of the potion; and although drowsy, and at first scarcely able to rouse himself, the startling nature of the intelligence speedily put new life into him. In a few moments the horses were saddled, and he was riding with his sons through the grey morning twilight to Teraya.

"I think I shall save her," said Amina in a low tone to her uncle, as he entered the room in which Tigranuhe was lying, with closed eyes, and in a state of exhaustion almost amounting to collapse—"or rather that she will save herself—for she retains her full consciousness, and I am simply obeying her direc-

[1] Christians.   [2] Muleteer.

tions. The violence of the paroxysms is certainly abating; the fear seems to me that she may not have strength to rally. It will be better that she is not excited by knowing that you are here. Zarifa," she continued, turning to her maid, " you can remain with her now, and give her the medicine as she asks for it. I can do nothing more for her just now, and I need a little rest after the terrible strain that this night has been."

" You need refreshment too, my daughter ; come to my room, and tell me what has happened while you take it."

Sheikh Mohanna listened attentively to Amina's recital of the events of the night, and after she had finished, remained thoughtful and silent for some moments.

" There is something in all this deeper than we can fathom," he said at length. " I much fear that there has been some collusion between Shibley and the Masollams. My absence was evidently arranged, and I have little doubt that my suspicion, when I woke from a sleep that seemed unnatural, that I had been drugged last night, was well founded. It was evident that Shibley never intended that I should be in a condition to take part in the discussion to which he invited me. You tell me that Daoud Effendi is not seriously wounded. Rest here, my child, while I go and see him. I would speak with him alone."

Masollam had just awoke from a troubled sleep. He was lying propped up with pillows, and he turned his eyes languidly upon the sheikh, without manifesting any emotion.

" Peace be upon you! I am glad to see you once again in my house, O Daoud Effendi, my old friend; but it grieves me much that it should be in such a condition, and under such circumstances."

" I have much to be thankful for, and I do not complain. God has dealt very mercifully with me," Masollam added after a pause, " for I have sinned against Him grievously. How is Tigranuhe? Will she live?"

" Amina is hopeful."

Masollam raised his eyes, then closed them, and for some moments his lips moved.

" I desire to confess to you," he said at length. " God wills it."

The old man then narrated the circumstances of Shibley's visit to Damascus. He

described the nature of the contract he had
entered into with Tigranuhe ; the complex
motives by which he was himself actuated in
his determination to thwart their designs ; his
substitute of the narcotic for the poison ; his
conviction that Tigranuhe had determined to
rid herself of his presence ; and the instinct of
self-preservation which had decided him to
anticipate her. He went on to narrate the
effect of Amina's visit upon him. How her
few words had shattered the hard shell, which,
under the influence of Tigranuhe and his own
uncontrolled passions, had for years past
gradually accreted round all that was origi-
nally pure and noble within him, until his
whole nature had become petrified, and he
retained but the outward mask or semblance
of what he once was. How for a moment, as
the petrifaction began as it were to melt, all
seemed chaos within, one idea alone crystal-
lising itself out of it, and this was, that he
must not attempt to save his own life by
taking Tigranuhe's, if she would abandon the
idea of the robbery she meditated. But when
she refused to do this, then it seemed as
though the means had been providentially put

into his hands by her own criminal act, and
he determined to use the poison she had de-
signed for another, on herself. He perceived
now that he had no justification for this act;
but his whole moral sense was too disturbed
at the time for him to see anything plainly.
He blindly followed the ruling instinct. But
ever since that supreme moment, the change
within him had been slowly but surely pro-
gressing. As a drowning man is said to pass
all the events of his life in rapid review during
his last moments of consciousness, so there had
been revealed within the last few hours to his
quickened moral sense, the influences which
had been operating for years past to distort it.
He could look back and analyse the processes
of this moral disintegration with a painful dis-
tinctness.

He could see how, by reason of glorying in
his own humility, he had become inflated with
the pride of Lucifer; how he had made the
profession of extreme disinterestedness a cloak
to conceal his avarice, and had become wealthy
in proportion as he had become skilled in the
art of obtaining money under false moral pretences; how like one of old he had let the

woman tempt him, and had absorbed the virus
of her poison, her insatiable ambition, her un-
rivalled power of deceit, her cruelty, her
malice and her jealousy; how — already an
arena of conflicting lusts and passion—he had
allowed a love, which in his infatuation he had
imagined pure and holy, to enter which domi-
nated all the rest, and paralysed all those
faculties and gifts which the ignorant call
supernatural, upon which his authority and
his great prestige had been based; how this
love had hurled him into violent collision
with the guardian influences of her he desired
to possess, operating on earth through Santalba
and Clareville, and how in the conflict which
followed, he was overthrown and vanquished;
how henceforth his very intellect began to
weaken, and he found himself gradually fall-
ing a helpless victim to her he called his wife.
All this he told Mohanna, with a lucidity and
a power of expression which proved to the old
sheikh that, with the restoration of his moral
fibre, his intellectual vigour was returning, and
that by the pistol-shot with which Tigranuhe
had attempted to take his life, she had, under
Providence, effected his salvation.

When he had finished, the old sheikh took Masollam's hand in both of his.

"What you have told me, O my friend," he said, "affects me more deeply than I can find words to express; the more especially as I, like yourself, have passed through the valley of the shadow since those early days when we used to open our thoughts to each other; but there is one who will feel it, if possible, more acutely than I do, whose sympathy for you ·will be as tender as that of a mother, in whose heart you will ever find a home. You know whom I mean."

"Yes," replied Masollam, gently bowing his head. "Santalba."

At this moment Sada appeared at the door.

"The Khateeb is here," she said, "and wishes to see you."

With a faint pressure of Masollam's hand the sheikh left him, and found the Khateeb in his outer apartment.

"I have come, O sheikh," he said, "to tell you what happened at Ain Ghazal while you were asleep last night, as it is a matter which somewhat perplexes me, in regard to which I would be glad to have some explanation."

"It was my intention," replied Mohanna, "to have paid you a visit for the purpose of talking to you about this very subject; I have therefore to thank you for having anticipated me."

The Khateeb then gave a very accurate report of the conversation which had taken place, and of Shibley's presentation of the matter.

"I feel obliged to you," said Mohanna, when he had listened to it, "for having insisted on a postponement of the question; the statement of Sheikh Shibley was, as you rightly conjecture, false in every particular. As he evidently did not desire the truth to be known, I will not now betray his confidence, the more especially as the subject will come up again before long in a very different form from what he anticipates. Meantime you would do me a service by keeping me informed as to his movements and designs, in so far as you are yourself aware of them, and, believe me, I shall not forget your loyalty and good faith on this occasion."

The Khateeb took his leave, and Sheikh Mohanna returned to Amina.

"Have you got the letter," he asked, "which you received from Santalba yesterday, just before I started for Ain Ghazal?"

The girl pulled a letter from her bosom. "This is not the one," she said, with a slight blush, as she was about to open it. "I have made a mistake; it is from Reginald Clareville. See, here is the letter from Santalba."

"When does he say that he expects to be here?"

"He hopes they will all four arrive here about the end of next month; that would be a month from now."

"It will be a time of suspense and possible difficulty for us, my child; I would they could have been here sooner—and yet we have no right to complain, for our dear friend allows himself no rest; it is scarce eight weeks since he left us, and we did not then expect him so soon."

"He says events are moving very rapidly in the interval, and indeed we see as much from the unexpected culminations of our own latest experiences. He must have felt we could get through this crisis without him."

"Then you suppose, by his hurrying so

much to get back to us, that there will be another in a month from now?"

"I do not say that. No one can really foresee the future, not even those who are not hampered with quite such gross bodies as we are, and have passed into another stage of existence. All that either they or we can do —if we have a little more insight than our neighbours have yet attained to—is to calculate probabilities with rather more accuracy. And now tell me about Daoud Effendi; I have not seen him since I bound up his wound."

Amina listened with great interest to Mohanna's narrative, not only of his conversation with Masollam, but with the Khateeb, for the sheikh had made it a point to conceal nothing from her, and she had been aware of the object of his visit to Shibley. She shuddered at the evidence which it all conveyed of the determination of the young sheikh to force on a union with her in spite of all obstacles. And the fact that one attempt involving so much treachery and crime had failed, only served to increase her anxiety— as well for the sheikh's life as for her own, for she was determined never to let Shibley obtain possession of her alive.

"What do you intend to do?" she asked.

"Of an active kind, nothing. It is important to conceal from Shibley what we know, especially as we have no means of bringing it home to him. Better to lull him into security by avoiding any act which may savour of hostility or even suspicion towards him. To make him desperate is to make him still more dangerous. We are now thoroughly warned, and have only to take the necessary measures of precaution, to keep ourselves well informed as to his movements, and to trust in the protection of Providence. He has never given us any reason to doubt it," added the sheikh, with a smile.

"You are right, uncle," said Amina. "I had a foolish momentary impulse of panic just now, but it is past. For us, what the world calls danger, does not exist."

CHAPTER XII.

THE KHATEEB COMES TO SHEIKH SHIBLEY'S AID.

To calm his own agitation, and distract his mind from the anxiety to which he was a prey after Sheikh Mohanna's hurried departure, Shibley mounted his horse and galloped off to recall the band whom he had sent to waylay the Masollams, and whose mission he now knew to be hopeless. He found them posted at the spot he had indicated, a lonely gorge, whence he had calculated escape would be impossible, if the travellers had been set upon from front and rear, as he had planned. His men reported that a few minutes previous to his arrival, a party, well armed and mounted, had passed through the gorge on their way to Teraya; that one of the Druses had ridden out to accost them, the others remaining in ambush, and had asked them whence they had come, and whither they were bound; and that they had replied they were on their way from Hasbaya to Tibnin, a reply which seemed to them suspicious, as there was a more direct route; that they were at the moment holding a consultation as to whether it would not be desirable to follow and watch them, when Shibley had himself arrived.

"You have done well," he said, "but there is no need for you to stay here, as I have just received intelligence that the travellers have abandoned their intention of leaving Teraya to-day. Return home, then, and I will none the less reward you liberally for the service you were prepared to render me."

"Traitors!" muttered Shibley between his teeth. "So they not only played me false in the matter of the poison, but were prepared to give me a fight for the treasure besides, if, as I suspect, these men come from Hasbaya to serve as an escort on their return journey." To make sure of this, Shibley made a rapid circuit, and when he had almost reached Teraya, wheeled sharply round and rode along the Hasbaya road, as though coming from the village. He soon met the party he was in quest of. Riding up to their leader, he inquired if he was on his way to Teraya to escort Daoud Effendi Masollam and his wife back to Hasbaya? On receiving an affirmative reply, he informed them that he had been requested by Daoud Effendi to tell them that, as the latter had determined to remain some days more at Teraya, their services would not be required; and, with his suspicions thus reduced to a certainty, he himself rode into Teraya, and alighted at the house of the Khateeb at the moment when the latter was absent on his visit to Masollam.

He met with a cold and gloomy reception from Afifi and her mother, for the Khateeb had reported the occurrences at Ain Ghazal, and the determination which Shibley had manifested to secure Amina for his bride. Shibley saw that at all hazards he must regain the friendship of this family as the last means which existed of obtaining information as to what was transpiring at Mohanna's house, and the disposition of the sheikh towards himself. He was tortured with anxiety to know how much the old man knew of his treachery; and

his main object in so speedily coming to the
Khateeb's was to persuade the latter, if possible, to keep silence as to what had passed
while the sheikh was asleep. When he heard
from Afifi that her father was at that moment
visiting Mohanna, he saw that he was too late,
and that he must at once invent explanations
which should satisfy the mother and daughter, and, if possible, win them back to his
interests.

"The Khateeb has told you what happened
at my house last night, I suppose," he remarked, "and my object in coming here now
is to explain it. You heard, no doubt, that I
consulted the sheikhs present in regard to
my marriage with Amina; I could not tell
them then what I can tell you now, what
my real motives are. You do not suppose
that I really care for a girl who despises her
religion and her people, and manifests an
especially strong aversion to me, the head
of her family. But perhaps you do not know
that she is enormously rich ; the possessor of
treasure, concealed in her uncle's house, which
would make the house of Zedaan the most
wealthy in the nation. It is this treasure,

not the girl, that I desire to obtain; for it is
not right that any woman should possess such
wealth. Her uncle, however, refuses to compel
her to part with it to those to whom it should
more properly belong, or even to consent to
her marriage with me, whereby I should without further difficulty enter into possession.
Once mine, I should lose no time in getting
rid of one whom I dislike as much as she
dislikes me; and," he added, with a tender
glance at Afifi, "I should follow my own
inclinations in taking a wife. But it is a
duty I owe, not only to my own family, but
to my people, not to let the vast sum of money
represented by these jewels slip away to the
pocket of some Franji upon whom the strange
girl has set her affection. With it I could
enrich all my relatives to the third and fourth
degree, and yet have abundant for myself; and
she whom I should make my wife," and he
again looked at Afifi, "would be the richest
woman of the nation."

The eyes both of mother and daughter
sparkled at this prospect, and Shibley perceived the impression this unexpected revelation was producing.

" Does my husband know anything of this ?" asked the wife of the Khateeb.

" No one knows of it yet; but it cannot long remain a secret, for last night the Jew from Damascus arrived with his wife, by whom Amina was brought up. They claim the treasure, and endeavoured to steal it during Sheikh Mohanna's absence; but it seems they quarrelled over the spoil, and tried to murder each other, and are both now lying at the point of death. But here comes the Khateeb; doubtless he will be able to give us the latest information."

But the Khateeb was rather in an unamiable mood, because he knew nothing. He had heard various wild rumours, and had expected that Sheikh Mohanna, in return for the information he had given him as to the occurrences at Ain Ghazal, would have taken him into his confidence, instead of which the old man had maintained a complete silence with regard to the tragedy which had taken place under his own roof, and the Khateeb had been too proud to allude to the subject. He listened at first moodily, but gradually with awakened interest, to Shibley's narrative; for the latter did not

conceal from him that, having reason to suspect the robbery, he had taken precautions to
arrest the thieves. He dwelt on the danger
of the loss to the nation of all this wealth, on
the lack of devotion ₌exhibited by Sheikh Mohanna to the interests of his family and race,
and finally promised the Khateeb to wed his
daughter, if he would co-operate with him in
obtaining possession of the jewels, either by
fair means or foul. Fair means meant marrying Amina first, and divorcing her afterwards;
and foul meant stealing the jewels, and going
off with them to the Jebel Druze.

The Khateeb, who was a man of caution
and deliberation, refused to give any hasty
pledge in the matter. He had won the confidence of Sheikh Mohanna so completely by
his recent conduct, that he could betray him
all the more easily whenever it became his
interest to do so. In the meantime, he re-
commended Shibley to return quietly home,
and avoid doing anything which should give
rise to fresh suspicion. He was sure, he said,
that his movements would be narrowly watched,
and therefore, whatever might be the plan
decided upon, it would require to be matured

and carried out with extreme secrecy and caution. The Khateeb being now thoroughly in possession of all the facts, said he would think them over, and in the course of a few days would ride over to Ain Ghazal, and tell Shibley the results.

With this assurance the young sheikh returned home somewhat relieved in his mind, and awaited events. On the following morning the Khateeb saddled his horse and set forth on a round of visits. He was away a fortnight, Shibley meanwhile tortured with impatience, and only obeying his instructions by the exercise of great self-control. At last he was gladdened one day by the entrance of the Khateeb. The latter now assured Shibley that the object of his journey had been to explain the situation to the sheikhs of a large circuit of villages. He had sounded them privately and in succession. He had explained to them how very much more important it was, now that Amina was known to be the owner of great wealth, that she should be compelled without delay to give in her adhesion to the Druse religion, and identify herself by marriage with the race to

which she belonged, than if she had been a
pauper; and there was not one who had not
seen it instantly in the same light. From
being an anomaly, and therefore rather a
nuisance than otherwise, she had become a
most valuable and cherished prize; and the
Khateeb skilfully directed the general indignation against Sheikh Mohanna for practically
proving false to his nation by not regarding
her in the same light. The discovery of
Amina's treasure had in fact been due to an
accident, whereas it was the evident duty of
her uncle to take measures from the first for
securing her jewels for the family, instead of
keeping their existence a secret from those
most interested in them. His reluctance to
force Amina to give in her adhesion to their
religion, his refusal even to consent to her
marriage with Shibley, all told against him,
especially in the minds of those who had
resented his assumption of having had a revelation of a secret interpretation of one of
the books of Hamzé, which was in many
respects unorthodox. Finally, the Khateeb
had had a secret meeting with several of
the sheikhs most hostile to Mohanna, in

which it had been agreed that he must be formally called to account, and not only give explanations of his conduct, but, under the pain of penalties provided in such cases by the religion, be required to coerce his niece into the proposed marriage with Shibley — a marriage much desired by the girl's own mother. Some of the leading sheikhs had agreed to make a secret propaganda in this sense, and when all was prepared, to notify Mohanna that a grand meeting was convened for a certain date, to take place at Teraya, on important questions affecting the interests of the nation, in the Khalweh, or church, which is the secret council chamber of the Druses on these occasions.

"As one or two of the sheikhs whose presence is the most necessary are absent from home," pursued the Khateeb, when he had finished this statement, "the meeting will necessarily be delayed for some days longer; but no harm can result from this; on the contrary, it will lull them into all the greater security. The fact that the thieves, who were caught, as I now understand, red-handed in their attempt to steal the jewels, are still kept

in the house as honoured guests, upon whom
both Sheikh Mohanna and his niece lavish
the greatest care and attention, is another
most suspicious circumstance which will have
to be inquired into."

"Do you think," asked Shibley, "that the
sheikh has any idea of the object of your late
journey?"

"It is impossible for me to be certain that
there may not be one who is sufficiently his
friend to give him a hint of it; but if so, he
has carefully concealed his suspicions from
me, for I called on him yesterday immediately
on my return.   There are various questions
pending in some of the villages, and I accounted for my journey by pretending that
I had gone upon invitation.   It therefore
caused him no surprise; and he took occasion
again to thank me for the part I took in the
discussion we had that night, when I suggested that the consideration of the whole
matter should be postponed.   As it turns
out," added the Khateeb, drily, "you are
likely to have more reason to thank me for
the course I adopted on that occasion than
he has."

"Yes, for it has enabled you to gain his confidence; but now that you are in possession of all the facts, you understand the haste I was in to bring matters to a conclusion, though, as we now see, it would have been premature."

The Khateeb was right in his conjecture; among those whom he had consulted in regard to the conduct of Sheikh Mohanna, there was one who was too good a friend of the old man not to keep him accurately informed of the conspiracy which was being hatched against him. Sheikh Suleiman was an ardent admirer, and a most devoted adherent and disciple, of Mohanna. He was a young man of an enthusiastic temperament and a devout mind, and had from his youth been attracted by those qualities in the sheikh to which his own nature furnished a willing response. He lost no time, therefore, in making a night journey to Teraya—for one of the most marked characteristics of the Druses is the secrecy with which all their operations are conducted; and Sheikh Suleiman considered that it was most important that the Khateeb should have no inkling that his treachery to Sheikh Mo-

hanna had been discovered by the latter.
Hence it was that the old sheikh was especially on his guard when he received the
Khateeb's visit, not to let him suppose that
he knew anything, while he cast about in
vain for some loophole of escape from the
toils which were being so subtly and silently
woven round him.

"I see only one way," he said, on discussing
the matter with Amina, "and that would be
to send you off swiftly and silently to some
Christian friends I have in Damascus, who
would take care of you until the arrival of
Girius Bey and your other friends from
Europe."

Amina shook her head. "For many reasons," she said, "such a scheme is impracticable. In the first place, Tigranuhe is too ill
to be moved; the nervous shock to her system
has produced some kind of creeping paralysis.
Have you remarked how indistinct her utterance is becoming, and with what difficulty she
can move her limbs? She told me last night
that she knew that she was going to lose all
power in them. It would be impossible to
move her in her present condition, and as

impossible for me to leave her. In the next place, if you allowed me to escape with my diamonds, how could you justify yourself to your people. Believe me, we are stronger united than separated, and shall not be abandoned in the hour of our need. Until we see a distinct avenue of escape opened, or find weapons put into our hands to meet this crisis, our duty is to await it in faith that we shall be protected by other means than those of our own devising. Let us thank God for the calm we are enjoying, even though the indications point to its being a treacherous one.

The old man bowed his head in acquiescence, and at this moment Masollam entered the room. He was so far recovered that he was able to move about, and spent most of his time in Tigranuhe's room watching by her bedside, and manifesting a tenderness which, if that invalid did not actively repel, she neither invited nor seemed to appreciate. If, in obedience to occult natural laws, occult mainly because of the blindness and prejudice which refuse to investigate them, phenomena termed miraculous can be produced, whereby the blind can be made to see, the

deaf to hear, the lame to walk, and the sick
to be healed—there is no reason why operations as wonderful and apparently miraculous,
of a moral kind, should not be performed by
the same or correlated laws, whereby the whole
nature undergoes a transformation, known to
theologians as " the casting out of devils,"
—the last well-authenticated instance having
occurred, according to them, in the case of
one Paul, who cast " a spirit of divination out
of a girl, who brought her master much gain
by soothsaying," some eighteen hundred and
thirty-three years ago.   It was some such
change as this that had been operated upon
Masollam, — partly through the agency of
Amina, and partly by reason of the shock which
he had sustained on the night when he himself
narrowly escaped death at the hands of Tigranuhe,—which left him bereft of his gifts, but
restored to his moral equilibrium ; a meek, sub-
dued old man, crushed beneath the load of the
memories by which he was haunted, but strong,
notwithstanding, in his determination to bear
it, and to make such reparation as lay in his
power to those whom he had despoiled and
deluded.   To this end he had been once more

using Amina as his amanuensis; and many of
those with whom Santalba had been so recently
in communication, now received, in a hand-
writing with which they were familiar, letters
dictated by Masollam, admitting the truth of
all that the Count had said in regard to himself, and furnishing unanswerable evidence of
his repentance by announcements of the arrangements he was making to pay them back
in full all that he had ever received at their
hands, though by so doing he would leave
himself a beggar.

"Not a beggar," Amina had said, when,
after a full calculation of his assets, it seemed
that such must be the result. "Not while
Count Santalba and I live, either in purse
or in love."

Neither she nor Sheikh Mohanna had
thought it necessary to take Masollam into
consultation over their own troubles, and the
dangers that were menacing them, fearing
to add to his burden; but as he entered, he
observed the anxious expression of the old
sheikh, and though nothing external betrayed
it, he was conscious of a slight mental agitation in Amina.

" You look troubled," he said, glancing from
one to the other. "I fear me that the continued presence of Tigranuhe and myself here
is a cause of embarrassment to you."

" By no means ; it is my presence here which
is a cause of the most extreme embarrassment
both to my uncle and myself, and all concerned," answered Amina.

" How so ? I only ask from sympathy, not
from curiosity."

" I feel as if I must tell him, uncle," said
Amina ; and she narrated all the circum-
stances of the plot in which Shibley and the
Khateeb were engaged.

" When do you expect this meeting to take
place ? "

" We do not know exactly ; it depends upon
the return of some sheikhs who have gone to
the Lebanon."

" And when do you expect Girius Bey ? "

" In about a fortnight from now, perhaps in
less."

" Did you not tell me that Clareville and
the Sebastian Hartwrights would accompany
him ? "

" Yes."

" Then send them a telegram from Damascus to hurry them, and manage to delay the
meeting until their arrival.   If you can do
this, and I am not speaking now in a spirit of
prophecy," and the old man smiled sadly, " but
from facts of which I have certain knowledge
—I say if you can manage this, you will successfully defy the whole Druse nation."

Sheikh Mohanna looked up surprised, and
somewhat incredulous.

" I cannot now tell you my reasons for
making such a positive assertion," said Masollam, with a strong emphasis; " but believe
me, I would not risk it if there was the
smallest doubt about it."

CHAPTER XIII.

AMINA ASSERTS THE RIGHTS OF WOMAN.

ON the day following this conversation, Santalba received a telegram, dated Damascus,
the result of which was, that the next evening
he left Paris for Switzerland, where he was
joined by Clareville and the Sebastian Hartwrights, proceeding thence by the most direct
route for Syria. The express messenger who
had carried this message to Damascus from Teraya had scarcely returned to Teraya with the
answer, announcing the departure of the party,
when Sheikh Mohanna was taken seriously ill,
and according to the custom on such occasions,
visitors flocked to his house with the view of
crowding round his bed. The Khateeb was one
of the earliest to present himself, and was much
surprised and offended at being received by

Amina, and informed that the sheikh's illness being one that required absolute quiet, she was compelled to refuse admittance to all visitors. This aroused a strong feeling of indignation against her throughout the village, and much strengthened the hands of the party with whom, either from jealousy or for some other reason, she was unpopular. Gratitude is too much mingled with suspicion to be a virtue among the Druses. Amina's devotion to the sick, her generosity with her purse, and her tender consideration for all with whom she was brought into contact, had rendered her, it is true, generally popular with the women; but the men all the more resented the presumption on the part of a woman which should venture to exclude them from the sick-room of the sheikh while they suspected her motives; and it required all Sada's influence and authority—which, as widow of their late sheikh, was considerable—to prevent them from forcing their way in. The Khateeb had the same morning received a message announcing the return of the sheikhs from the Lebanon, whose arrival had alone delayed the assembling of the council at Teraya; and angry and

suspicious, he rode over to Ain Ghazal to consult Shibley. That young man, who had been
fuming with impatience, saw in the incident
an excuse for forcing his own presence on
Amina, and decided, as a relation of the family, to claim his right of access to Mohanna;
while it was agreed that the Khateeb should
pay a visit to the newly arrived sheikhs, to
whom he had not had an opportunity of explaining the nature of the case in regard to
which their decision was desired.

Shibley was anxious to see Mohanna for
several reasons : one was, to judge for himself
of the nature and gravity of his illness; another was, to endeavour to explain his own
conduct on the occasion of the meeting which
had taken place at his house, and, so far as
might be possible, restore himself to the good
graces of the sheikh; and a third was, to
discover the motives which induced the latter
to keep the Masollams as permanent guests
in his house. His mind was tortured with
suspicion and worried by conjecture at this
totally unaccountable proceeding. He had
remained entirely in the dark as to what
really had happened on that eventful night.

It had leaked out that Masollam had been
wounded by a pistol-shot, and that Tigranuhe
had been at the point of death; but whether
they had actually attempted the robbery of
the diamonds or not, he was ignorant. He
had indeed assumed, as he had told the Khateeb, that they had quarrelled over the spoil,
but he had no assurance of this; and if it
were not so, the spoil was still there, and they
were in the house with it, and might at any
moment take advantage of the opportunities
which their protracted visit must have afforded them, to appropriate it and make their
escape. Tigranuhe's illness might be assumed;
he had heard that Masollam was rapidly recovering. At any moment they might dis-
appear with the prize. The very thought
made him tremble. Certainly it was a matter
that must be looked to, and one in regard to
which he could only satisfy himself by a personal visit. It was evident he had nothing
to fear. More than a fortnight had elapsed
since he had unsuccessfully attempted the
sheikh's life, and misrepresented to the assembled company the object of their meeting; but a profound stillness had reigned

ever since at Teraya. At all events, a visit there now would ensure him an interview with Amina; and he was possessed by such an insatiate craving to see her again that it was worth any risk; and it would also give him an opportunity of a private conversation with Sada, from whom he hoped to extract all the information he thirsted for with regard to the Masollams. Indeed he thought it just possible he might see Daoud Effendi himself. It was therefore with a heart beating violently under the influence of passion, nervousness, curiosity, and a desire for vengeance, that Shibley rode across the *meidan* to the entrance of Sheikh Mohanna's house at Teraya. After the manner of Druses, he walked in unannounced, and was actually in the sick man's room before any one had seen him. The sheikh was asleep, and Amina was sitting by his side reading, when, hearing a step, she looked up, and saw her cousin within two paces of her.

With infinite coolness and presence of mind she rose gently, placed her finger on her lip, and softly left the room, beckoning Shibley to follow her.

She led him across the court to the guest's room, and motioned to him to be seated.

"I have been expecting you," she said. "I was sure you would come when you heard that the sheikh was ill. Indeed he has been surprised that you have never been to see him since the night he dined with you."

Her perfect calmness, and a certain air of condescension, which would have irritated Shibley even in a sheikh of rank superior to himself, exasperated him beyond measure in this girl, who seemed placed above him on some lofty pedestal, at a height to which he could never hope to attain. His first instinct was one of rage, and a desire to hurl her at his feet and crush her beneath them; and then another and softer feeling stole over him, one which he had never experienced for any human being, and of the existence of which he had been ignorant. As he gazed at her in silence—for he was too much overcome by this conflict of emotion to speak—it grew in strength until, to his own astonishment, he felt an almost uncontrollable desire to throw himself at her feet and worship her. As he looked at the dainty slippers peeping from beneath the folds of the full trousers, it would be a greater pleasure, he thought, to be trampled under those tiny feet than to obey his own first cruel instinct. Amina kept. her large calm eye fixed upon him, as a keeper does upon a tiger which he is taming. Shibley wiped the drops of perspiration from his brow.

"You know," he said at length, in a suppressed tone, "why I could not come. You brought Fadda here to prevent me."

"I brought Fadda here because you treated her as no brave man should treat a woman. I was ashamed that my father's cousin's son could be so base and cruel, and I made her the only reparation in my power."

"Silence, girl!" exclaimed Shibley. "Who are you that you should dare to use such language to me? Another word, and I will strike you to the earth."

"Is that the way Druse men win the affections of the women they love?" said Amina, rising from her seat.

"It is the way Druse men make the women they love obey them."

" And hate and despise them if they are true women," added Amina, with a glance of supreme contempt as she moved towards the door.

Shibley's impulse was to endeavour to retain her by force, but he saw that she would escape him, and he still had enough self-possession to perceive that the scandal which would result from a pursuit could in no way advance his ends. It was not by such means that he would obtain the information he desired.

" Stop, Amina ! " he cried ; " you are different from Druse women, and I was wrong to treat you as one."

Amina paused. She was anxious, if possible, to gain ascendancy over this savage nature, and not to drive him out of the house like an infuriated wild beast.

" Now that you understand that," she said, turning to him, and again fixing her eye on his, " perhaps we shall get on better. I do not on that account forget that you are the nearest relation I have on my father's side, and, believe me, my earnest desire is that we should remain good friends ; but I will leave

the room and refuse ever to see you again,
unless you promise to remember what you
have just said, that I am different from Druse
women, in that I will not submit to be threat-
ened, and will not permit you to treat me
with disrespect."

"One would imagine," said Shibley, grimly,
"that you thought yourself man's equal."

"In every respect," returned Amina; "and
from the exhibition you have just afforded
of your own manhood, I perceive that some
Druse men are inferior to the women of other
nations."

Shibley had never seen a Spanish bull-fight,
but if he had, he might have likened himself
to the bull, and Amina to the *toreador;* her
stabs maddened him, but he felt powerless to
retaliate. He could only keep her with him
by submission, and her presence was what
he craved for more than aught else at the
moment.

"At all events," he said with a short laugh,
"Druse women have this in common with
those of other nations, they have sharp
tongues, and often talk nonsense. Had
Sheikh Mohanna been instructing you in our

religion, as he promised, you would know that it does not allow us to consider women as the equals of men. However, as there are none of them like you, I will consent to make an exception in your favour. And now that we are good friends again, tell me what is the matter with Sheikh Mohanna."

"He has an attack of fever—he has, indeed, never been thoroughly well since the night he spent with you. He must have eaten something then that disagreed with him."

Shibley shot a sharp suspicious glance at her.

"How are your other patients?" he asked.

"Daoud Effendi is much better. His wife, I fear, will never recover; she is still too ill to be moved."

"What is the nature of her illness?"

"You would not understand my description of it if I gave it you."

"Do you know how it was produced?" persisted Shibley.

"By an overdose of a very powerful medicine. Why are you so interested?"

"Oh, I have heard so many rumours about an attempt to steal some diamonds, and a

quarrel which resulted from it, that I was
anxious to know the truth."

"The Druses seem to me very fond of
gossip," said Amina. "And now I must leave
you for a moment, for perhaps my uncle may
need me."

"I will come with you," said Shibley, rising.

"No, you won't; you will sit here, and take
your first lesson of obedience to a woman. I
will return in a moment." And Amina tripped
off, leaving Shibley hesitating between in-
subordination and what he considered indignity. He decided in favour of the latter.
In a few moments Amina returned, followed
by Zarifa, bearing refreshments. She had
taken the opportunity of making all safe.
Sada and Fadda she had posted with the
sheikh. She had warned both of Shibley's
presence, and extracted from them a promise
not to leave Mohanna's side while he was in
the house. Masollam, when he heard of the
visit, was only too anxious to avoid meeting
the young sheikh, and remained with Tigranuhe. Amina therefore returned with her
mind at ease, and for an hour exerted all her
power of fascination to reduce her cousin to

that condition of abject slavery, the fetters of
which the Western lover delights to rivet upon
himself, but which were as new and irksome
to Shibley as harness to a zebra. At the end
of that time he rode away in no respect wiser
than he came in regard to all he desired
to know, feeling, nevertheless, delightfully
soothed and comforted. His had been a gay
youth; he had been married twice, and although flirtation is attended with considerable
difficulty among the Druses, he had managed
to indulge the tender passion—at great risk,
it is true—in forbidden directions; but what
he felt now was so foreign to all previous experience, that he was unable to do more than
revel in it as a new sensation. His faculties
were too uncultured, and his perceptions too
dense, to enable him to attempt analysis. He
did not know that the subtle joy which seemed
to flood his being, arose from an unconscious
element of purity, which he derived from
Amina, but which had never entered into the
composition of any love he had felt for woman
before. For she had been giving him love—
not that of a woman for her lover, but that
love which God furnishes to those who live for

the whole race, and who believe that His love
alone put forth through them can save it.
So Shibley rode home, trying to read the
riddle that he had become to himself—won-
dering at the strength and the character of
that devotion with which a woman had inspired him, and the sweetness of which seemed
to increase just in proportion as he elevated
her above himself in his own estimation, and
invested her with attributes which made her
worthy of his worship. What was strangest
of all was, that he was conscious that in proportion as he did this, he seemed to rise
instead of sink in his own self-respect. To
exalt the woman he loved above himself, appeared to him now something not to be
ashamed of, but to glory in; and this was so
entirely opposed to all his preconceived notion
of the relation of the sexes, that he tried to
combat it; but as this only had the effect of
rendering him miserable, he violated the prejudices of his nature and the teaching of his
religion, and was happy. Had Shibley been
a philosopher, he might perhaps have come to
the conclusion that no moral progress was possible without violations of this sort.

"I shall be glad to see you again whenever you like to come," Amina had said when
they parted; "and you need not be afraid of
meeting Fadda, for I shall take care that on
these occasions she is always by my uncle's
bedside."

Amina had two motives in making this
speech; one was to keep Shibley away from
the sheikh, to whom his presence could only
be painful after what had happened, and who
really had very little the matter with him.
In fact, his illness had only been definitely
decided upon when it was certain, from the
message that had arrived from Paris, that it
need not be made to last more than a fortnight, and partook therefore of the nature of
that complaint to which statesmen and diplo-
mats are especially liable. Amina's second
reason for inviting Shibley to come and see
her was as strategic as her uncle's illness. She
hoped to acquire an influence over him, which,
should occasion demand, she might use to procure delay, or, at all events, to moderate the
violence of his designs against herself. She
would have shrunk from venturing upon so
bold a course, had it not been for the near ap-

proach of rescue in the shape of Santalba and Clareville. As it proved, her calculations were not misplaced. Shibley was only too glad of the opportunities thus afforded of *tête-à-têtes* with his cousin, and of the pleasure which he derived from them. He troubled himself neither about his uncle's illness nor the Masollams' designs. Another world was being opened out to him—a world of new emotions, of vague yearnings, of budding aspirations. The consciousness began to dawn upon him that there was nothing about him worthy of her he loved. His inferiority was no longer an admission made to satisfy her, in which he himself did not believe, but a stubborn reality, which all his vanity could not deny. A new motive for existence had burst upon him— one which the wildest flights of his unenlightened imagination would never have suggested — and this was to win the respect of a woman. He saw now he could not win her love without. Hitherto it had mattered not to him whether the woman whom he desired to make his wife loved him or not. She was his slave, and had to do his bidding; his own happiness was in no way affected by demonstrations of affection on her part, while, by the custom of his people, all outward show of tenderness on his was accounted an unworthy weakness. Now, in defiance of this prejudice, he began to long for an occasion when he might outwardly show himself deferential to Amina, if by so doing he might win her love, without which he felt that his union with her would lose all its charm. The change which in so short a time seemed stealing over him puzzled the Khateeb exceedingly; while Shibley's almost daily visits to Teraya so outraged his notions of propriety, that he felt called upon to remonstrate with him, more especially as Afifi had discovered that these visits were made exclusively to Amina, and that he had never been allowed admittance to the room of the sheikh.

"This illness of Sheikh Mohanna is suspicious," he said to him one day; "I believe it is merely assumed for the sake of gaining delay."

"Possibly," replied Shibley, who was now in no hurry to precipitate the storm he had himself conjured up.

"Then why don't you insist upon seeing him and judging for yourself?"

"Because Fadda is always there, and you know I cannot meet her."

"Know you not that it is as great an outrage of propriety to meet Amina alone almost daily, as you are doing, as to meet Fadda? Our friends, when they assemble, may have your conduct as well as Sheikh Mohanna's to consider, if you are not careful. This girl, with her foreign ways, is making a fool of you, as she has already of Sheikh Mohanna."

"She would make a fool of you too, if you saw as much of her as I do," said Shibley.

The Khateeb frowned. "This is trifling," he said, "and an insult to our friends, who have been notified of the reason we have invited them to meet here, and are waiting for the summons. I for one will be no longer a party to delay. I will at once request their attendance at my house, when we will discuss the position of the whole family, yourself included, whom this girl's presence has so strangely disturbed."

"You are right," said Shibley, suddenly changing his manner; "I have been weak and foolish, and am being hoodwinked. Thank you, old friend, for your good advice. I perceive this thing must not longer be delayed; but, as he is ill, it had better take place at Sheikh Mohanna's, and not in the Khalweh. It is right, however, that he have notice of it, so that he may order the necessary preparations to be made."

"Well, see to it at once," said the Khateeb; "and let an early day be fixed without delay."

Shibley hurried to Amina. "A messenger has arrived at the Khateeb's," he said, "from some of the sheikhs of the neighbouring villages, notifying their wish to meet here at an early day to discuss some matters of importance."

"Do they wish to meet at the Khalweh or here?"

"Here."

"Will the fourth day of the week do? To-day is the first; my uncle is recovering so rapidly that I have no doubt by that day he will be able to receive them in person. Before then I do not think it would be possible."

"I have no doubt, in that case, that it can be fixed for that day."

Amina had received through Carabet a tele-

gram announcing the safe arrival of the travellers at Beyrout, and calculated that on Tuesday
night, or at least in the course of Wednesday,
they would be at Teraya.

"Do you know what are the matters which
the sheikhs are coming here to consider?"
she asked.

Shibley hesitated a moment. "No," he said
at length.

"I do," she said calmly; "and as it is a
matter which affects all the family so much,
it is important that I do not lose any time in
telling my uncle. He will see how necessary
it is for him to make haste and get well, so I am
afraid I must ask you to take leave of me for
to-day." And she added gravely, "I am sure,
considering the object of this assembly, you
will agree with me that, in order not to give
more occasion for complaint as to all our pro-
ceedings than is necessary, it will be well for
you to suspend all further visits to me until
after it has taken place. I trust," she concluded, with a look full of meaning, "that nothing will occur then to prevent our meeting
afterwards on the same friendly terms that

we have been doing lately;" and with a salutation of more than common cordiality, Amina tripped away, leaving Shibley more convinced than ever that he had lived all his life in a delusion upon the important subject of woman.

CHAPTER XIV.

•

A PARTY OF RESCUE FROM THE WEST ARRIVES AT TERAYA.

LATE on the following Tuesday evening, there arrived at Teraya a cavalcade consisting of four foreigners, with their servants and baggage-animals. They rode so silently through the village in the darkness, that, except for the barking of dogs, there was nothing to indicate the approach of so unusual a party; and in fact the next day was far advanced before it came to the Khateeb's ears that some Franj had arrived at Sheikh Mohanna's. Santalba and his three friends had been joined at Beyrout by Carabet, in obedience to instructions which had been sent to him by Masollam; and the Armenian was thus at length afforded the opportunity of gratifying a curiosity which the prolonged absence

of the Masollams had severely tried. Since the
first letter from Amina, announcing his sister's
severe illness, he had received messages from
the Master, in which the latter informed him
of his intention of making a prolonged stay at
Teraya, and directed him to proceed to Beyrout and hold himself in readiness to accompany Count Santalba, and the party whose
acquaintance he had already made in England,
to Teraya. He was excessively puzzled by
instructions which implied a reconciliation for
which he could not account; but he was too
well trained to question them, although his
sister's silence suggested matter for doubt and
anxiety—nor did anything fall from Santalba
or any of the others of the party in the course
of their ride which tended to enlighten him.
Indeed he was himself the first to inform
them of the presence of the Masollams at
Teraya. Amina had confined herself, in a
letter which met them at Beyrout, to saying
that she looked anxiously for their arrival and
aid in matters which could better be explained
by word than by letter, and they had pushed
on without delay under Carabet's guidance.
And now, as Clareville looked up at the lofty

beetling cliff, with the outline of the large
irregular building which appeared to clamber
up its steep flank, faintly defined against it in
the gloom of the night, and remembered that
this was the birthplace of her he loved best on
earth, and was now her home, it became invested in his eyes with a tender and mysterious charm; and as he thought of its
inmate as of one menaced by an imminent
danger, and of the appeal from her which had
summoned him to her rescue, he felt like some
paladin of old plunging into strange lands,
and confronting unknown perils in defence of
youth and beauty. It was the first introduction to the East of Reginald, as well as of
Florence and Sebastian, and their arrival by
night beneath the frowning precipices of the
Teraya cliffs was well calculated to impress
the imagination. Florence shuddered as she
felt the influence of the wildness of the sur-
roundings: the marvel to her was not that
Amina should be in danger now, but that in
such a spot she could ever have considered
herself in safety.

The inmates of the strange abode which the
travellers were now straining their eyes

through the darkness to examine, had evidently been apprised of their approach, for lights began to flit about on the face of the cliff, and to travel rapidly down to its base, and here as they reached the foot of the long flight of stairs, they found assembled Sheikh Mohanna and his sons, Sada, and Amina. It was perhaps as well that the hour was one unpropitious for spectators, for Druse *convenances* would have been shocked at the extravagant delight exhibited by Amina at once more meeting her friends, and her enthusiastic demonstrations of it. It was natural that she should kiss Santalba—that she had done ever since her infancy; and that she should take Florence in her arms and twine them round her in a tender caress; and that in the cordial welcome with which she greeted both Reginald and Sebastian, she should remember that they came to her as her saviours as well as her guests. Although the travellers were tired, they would not retire to rest until their curiosity was satisfied in regard to the danger impending over Sheikh Mohanna and Amina; and a solemn conclave was held in Sheikh Mohanna's room, which lasted until the small hours of the

morning, in the course of which Amina gave
a narrative of the stirring events of the past
few weeks, and of the point to which matters
had culminated; of the nature of the meeting
which was to be forthwith held at Teraya by
the sheikhs and Okâls, in which her own fate
was to be decided; and of the assurance of Masollam that no decision of theirs could avail
against the influences which Santalba had it
in his power to bring to bear against it.

"He was right," said the Count, calmly
turning to Sheikh Mohanna and repeating in
Arabic what Amina had just said. "Strange
as it may seem to you, you may leave the
whole question with confidence in my hands
—though I am a stranger to your nation—
for reasons which I will privately explain to
you to-morrow. And now we can all retire
to our beds with our minds not only at rest,
but in a spirit of deep gratitude for this new
manifestation of our Father's care for those
who live only to serve Him, and for the
especial favour He has shown us in the restoration to reason of our beloved friend
Daoud Effendi Masollam, whom I yearn once
more to clasp in my arms."

While this was taking place in Mohanna's room, Carabet had been closeted with the Master; and after hearing from his lips the tragic incidents of their first night at Teraya, and of the change which had been operated thereby upon his own nature, had been introduced by him to his sister's bedside.

Carabet was shocked at a change of another kind which he perceived had taken place here: the keen and intelligent eye had become dim and apathetic; the features, always sharply defined, were now peaked and haggard; the cheeks and forehead furrowed with deep wrinkles; the utterance had become thick, and so indistinct as to be scarcely intelligible; and the hands, almost transparent from their thinness, lay apparently powerless upon the coverlet.

"You see now," whispered Masollam, " one reason why it was impossible for us to have returned to Damascus. That she is alive at all is due to the unremitting care and attention of that angel who has restored me to reason, and who sheds a life-giving influence upon all those who come within the range of it."

Carabet was watching his sister's face while
he was listening to Masollam; and although
the latter spoke in so low a tone as to be
inaudible to the invalid, he distinctly saw her
mouth twitch into a scornful smile.

"There at least is one," he said to himself,
"who, if she has been restored to life, has not
been restored to reason."

Masollam seemed to read what was passing
in his friend's mind, and sighed heavily.

"It is true," he said, "that from our finite
point of view, there are cases in which the
prolongation of existence appears but a doubt-
ful boon, which only seems to render the frail
organism a more convenient tenement for those
spirits of evil which had taken possession of
it during bodily health; but who can judge of
those mysterious inner processes, which come
into more powerful operation just in the degree in which the vitality of the outer particles
—of that gross external crust which we call
the body — weakens? That poor emaciated
frame is at this moment the arena of a terrific
spiritual conflict: the moral victory, it is possible, can only be won at the cost of physical
life; while, on the other hand, natural exist-

ence may be prolonged by the agency most destructive to moral progress. But our knowledge is too finite to enable us to judge of the deep internal causes which produce these varied effects. I am myself an instance of an exactly opposite experience. My bodily functions weakened in proportion as my spiritual insanities increased; whereas now, just in the degree in which I am regaining moral tone does my natural health improve, and do all my powers strengthen."

Carabet found little consolation in this exordium. He was really attached to his sister, and was unable altogether to overcome a natural feeling of animosity against the hand that had stricken her down. He turned gloomily away; it seemed for the moment as if his whole existence had been a failure, all his aspirations, myths, and all those in whom he had trusted, frauds. He felt inclined to doubt whether there was a God worth loving, a moral standard worth living for, or a world worth trying to save; and in this unsatisfactory frame of mind he sought the mattress that had been spread for him, and like many others of the inmates of the house that night, was too much agitated and troubled in his mind to win the repose to which, after the labours of the day, he was fairly entitled.

"Have you any idea," asked Clareville, when he found himself alone with Amina next morning, "what is the nature of the influence which Santalba can bring to bear upon these Druses in their meeting to-morrow, in the efficacy of which he seems so confident?"

"No, indeed," returned Amina; "and so strange does it seem to me, that had I not learned from experience how thoroughly his assurances are to be trusted, I should myself be disposed to doubt his power. He and my uncle are at this moment in deep consultation."

"From what has transpired, however," said Clareville, " it would seem as though the general result of the experiment of this return to your own people has not been very successful."

"On the contrary, all new experience is knowledge gained. It was necessary that I should come here and live among my own people,—to learn their character and the nature of their prejudices, to discover their virtues, and probe their weaknesses, in order to find out how they may best be reached; by what methods, without using one set of dogmas as a battering-ram wherewith to demolish another set, new and higher ideas of daily life and duty and social observances may be instilled into them by love and by example. And strange as it may seem to you, considering the position in which you find me placed, the result is not discouraging. There is a curious unrest among them, an expectation of a new development, which takes the form, in their minds, of the reincarnation of Hakeem; they are, in fact, like the Jews, expecting their Messiah, and though they have prophecies indicating the form this manifestation is to take, and the signs which are to precede it, various interpretations of an occult nature are given to these prophecies. Thus the armies, consisting of four millions of Chinese, which are to herald his approach, are not supposed by the more highly initiated to mean living men but spiritual armies—the Chinese being the symbolical term used for such of the "initiated," after they have passed into the other world, as shall have been found

worthy to be enrolled in the advent hosts of
the mighty Lord Hakeem; and I find from
my uncle that among the Uwahid, or most
deeply versed in the mysteries, there are dif-
ferences of opinion in regard to these symbolical interpretations, and that some go so far
as to assert that Hakeem will not appear in
person but in spirit, and will take possession
of the hearts of all men as the Lord of
Love, and that the submission of all the
princes of Christendom and Islam to him,
means the union in love of the creeds that
now live by reason rather of the hatred than
of the love that is in them—and that the massacre of the infidels means the massacre of the
evil passions which are in men, by the arm
of the Lord Hakeem, who is Love. Then
will come the universal reign of love, for
which a few of the best of the Druses, among
them my uncle, are passionately longing.
But what is the most remarkable is, that they
all believe that England contains many members of their sect; and you will find, if you
travel among them, that one of the first questions you will be asked is, whether there are
many Unitarians or Muwahideen in England?

When you say that there are not, they smile
incredulously, believing either that you wish
to conceal the fact, or that you are ignorant
of it, but it in no way affects their own firm
convictions in the matter. And the reason for
this is, that it is by the English Druses that
the immediate advent of the Messiah is to
be announced; and they will come bringing
presents to their Eastern brethren; but they
will only be known and recognised, in the
first instance, by certain of the initiated, for
the nation is not yet prepared to receive all
the light which these English Druses will
bring. It will therefore have to be tempered,
so as to dawn upon them gradually. And the
effect of it will be to make it clear to them
that before their Lord of Love can come, they
must erect a Temple of Love in which he may
be worshipped, and that this Temple of Love
will consist of four spiritual buildings, one in-
side of the other. The inmost building is the
heart. When, after long and painful conflict,
the Lord of Love has ejected from the heart
all that opposes Him, then the second building, by which it is enclosed, may be reared.
It is composed of the family, or such members

of it as, having built within their hearts the
Temple of Love, are now fitted to be the
family temple of the Lord of Love. The
third Temple of Love, which encloses these
other two, is the National Temple of the Lord
of Love, composed of all the families in the
Druse nation who have a family temple.
And the last and grand structure, which encloses all the others, is the Universal Temple,
which will be the consequence of the example
set by the Druse nation to other nations, who,
seeing the beauty and excellence of the effort
and its results, will forthwith endeavour to
imitate them, until finally the Universal
Temple will be reared, pervaded, and domin-
ated by the Lord of Love."

"And are you and I to inaugurate the
Druse millennium?" asked Reginald, with a
smile, looking up into Amina's glowing face.

"If the Druse millennium means the world's,
and if that can only be brought about by the
efforts of individuals upon it, I do not see that
the magnitude of the task constitutes a reason
why some one should not begin it."

"I suppose we must begin with the family,"
said Reginald.

Amina glanced at him sharply, for she thought she detected a suspicion of levity in his tone.

"I speak in all seriousness," he added, gravely.

"I do not yet know," she said, very softly, and placing her hand in his, "what you have achieved during these months that have elapsed since we met. Does the Lord of Love reign in your heart, not for me, but for the human race, which transcends all feeling for individuals, or family, or country, which seems to bind you up indissolubly with its destiny as a whole, so that you feel that you cannot rise independently of it, but can only rise with it, in the degree in which you feel that individually you are as it were shouldering the whole human burden, sympathising with its miseries, and acutely suffering in your own person from its distracted condition? Can you paraphrase those lines of Shakespeare and say—

" 'The world is out of joint; O blessed love !
That I was ever born to set it right' ?"

"I have gone into the depths to try and

learn the lesson," he answered. "See, here come Sebastian and Florence; they descended with me. Amina wants to know what we have been doing with ourselves since we parted," he said, turning to Sebastian.

"Florence had got all her plan cut and dried. She elaborated it as soon as it was decided we were to be married," said Sebastian, in reply to this appeal, "and had come to the conclusion that in order to sympathise with the sufferings of the poor, we must endeavour as far as possible to adopt their mode of life, if only for a time; and immediately on my release from the asylum, she proposed to me a very peculiar species of honeymoon. As you may remember, two hours after our wedding we started for the Continent. Florence did not even want you to know what our plan was, so I kept it a secret from everybody but Reginald and Santalba, whose assistance was necessary. The latter knew the contractor of a short line of railway that is being constructed in Switzerland, and begged him to give me employment as a deserving navvy out of work, with a young wife to support. We invested in some raiment appropriate to our condition. I allowed

myself just money enough to take me to my
destination third class, lest I should be tempted
into luxuries, and on the third day entered on
my work with a pick and shovel at two francs
a-day. Florence got taken into a washer-
woman's establishment, and spent most of her
day drubbing people's linen on the stones by
the side of the lake. As soon as Reginald
had seen you off from Paris he joined us;
but thanks to a better biceps than I have,
he commanded 25 centimes a-day higher pay.
Though our experiences did not last so long
as we intended, in consequence of Santalba
suddenly arriving and carrying us off with
him here, it was enough to make us realise
the hardships and sufferings of those who
have barely enough to live upon, and to
whom a few days' ill health means starvation.
I was laid up with rheumatism for a week,
during which time I was entirely dependent
for subsistence upon the earnings of Florence
and Reginald. We had determined to die
sooner than come upon any other funds than
those earned, and it is that absolute depend-
ence upon his daily health that makes the
labourer's life so precarious. We laid our-

selves out, so to speak, to be brought into
contact with misery, and we had not to seek
far to find it.   It was the old story, familiar to
those who work among the poor; but painful
though the experience of philanthropists may
be, it is nothing to that of being so poor yourself that you can do nothing to relieve the
misery round you, and of being compelled to
live among vice, and sickness, and squalor, as
though you were part and parcel of it.   Reginald lost so much flesh sitting up with sick
people all night, giving them half his food,
and having to work all day besides, that his
biceps no longer gave satisfaction, and he was
docked his extra 25 centimes."

" The moral ground he was breaking up was
stiffer than the material," said Amina, with a
smile.   " He was tunnelling through prejudices as well as through rocks, and levelling
himself down to other people, and levelling
other people up to him, making the crooked
ways straight and the rough places smooth;
and more than that, by the loving contact
you were both maintaining with mother earth,
and that Florence was keeping up on the lake
bank, you were all purifying your organisms

of gross magnetic elements which you had acquired in the fashionable world, and which had impeded the growth of pure and divine life within you. I did not know what you had been doing; but the moment I touched you when you arrived, I felt that a subtle change had taken place in those finer essences which at The Turrets were so charged with a force of fashionable filth as to be at times almost intolerable. I do not mean that you were in any way responsible for it; but it is no more possible for people to steep themselves in society without absorbing some of its poison, and incorporating it into the system to such a degree that highly sensitised organisms can be conscious of its existence, than it would be for them to wade through a sewer and not offend their delicate olfactory nerves."

"Oh," exclaimed Florence, "how very dreadful! and was I really so very offensive to you, dear, in the days when you first knew me?"

"People whom one loves, and whom one is working to save, are never offensive in one sense, though they may be in another; but

MASOLLAM :

you are pure and sweet now, my darling, and
we will not look back upon those dreadful
days when we all suffered so much, but rather
to the brighter time and the holy work that is
in store for us. See, there is a party winding
up the valley towards the village. I wonder
who they can be."

At this moment Sheikh Mohanna and Santalba joined the group assembled in the upper
court.

" Ah," said Mohanna, " they are my two
friends, Sheikh Mahmoud and Sheikh Ibrahim. I thought," he added, with a sly twinkle
of his eye, " as I am to receive so many of
Sheikh Shibley's friends here to-morrow, I
would take the opportunity of inviting one
or two of my own."

" They both hold the view that I was
explaining to you of the Druse millennium,"
said Amina in a low tone to Reginald, " and
are among the most learned of our people,
and stanch friends of my uncle."

For the rest of the afternoon Sheikh Mohanna and Santalba were employed in receiving their friends in confidential interviews.
First, they had a long private talk with the

two newly arrived shcikhs, then with Reginald and Amina, then with Sebastian and Florence, and finally with Masollam and Sada. In fact it was evident that a very important subject was under discussion, the nature of which will appear in the next chapter.

CHAPTER XV.

THE GRAND COUNCIL.

THE sheikhs began to arrive at an early hour on the following day at Teraya, meeting in the first instance at the house of the Khateeb, to which Shibley had already repaired in a somewhat uneasy frame of mind. It is certain that, could he have anticipated the friendly relations he had now established with his cousin, he would have trusted rather to his own fascinations and persuasion to advance his suit, than to the council he had been the means of convoking to compel her acquiescence in it. He might with perseverance and docility have won a willing bride. It is true that he must have forfeited a great amount of his own self-respect, have done violence to the prejudices of his race and his religion, and, above all, to the tyrannical impulses of his own nature; but it need only have been for a time. When once he had won the prize, the sacrifices he had made for that purpose would no longer be required of him, and he could have reasserted his own manhood and independence; whereas the step he was now taking would lose him all the ground he had won. Amina would violently resent this interference with her liberty, and the attack which it involved upon her uncle. While he was painfully uncertain whether the facts were sufficient to sustain the charges he proposed to bring against that venerable man, one thing was certain, to hesitate under the circumstances was to be lost. He had, in his desperation and his impetuosity, chosen his own battle-field and his own weapons, and the only course open to him now was to make the best of them. Things had gone so far that it was as much the interest of the Khateeb to carry the matter through successfully, as it was his own; while he knew that the personal feeling of jealousy of several of the other Sheikhs was such that they would strain every point to its utmost against Mohanna.

"I hear," said Shibley to the Khateeb, "that Sheikhs Mahmoud and Ibrahim arrived here yesterday. Sheikh Mohanna must have had sufficient warning of our intended meeting to have had time to invite them. They are men of such weight that our task will no longer be a simple one."

"It was your own fault," retorted the Khateeb, "for allowing that white-faced girl to beguile you with stories of her uncle's illness, and make you lose valuable time by amusing you with private interviews. The two sheikhs are not the only new visitors who have arrived. Girius Bey and three other Franj—two men and a woman—are also there."

This intelligence excited in Shibley's breast a most violent spasm of jealousy. He was convinced, as Tigranuhe had assured him, that Santalba was his rival, and this belief had been confirmed by sundry affectionate allusions which Amina had made to her friend in the course of their conversations, and by his own observations on the occasion of their first arrival. It was evident that the opportune appearance on the scene of this hated foreigner was to be accounted for by the fact that his cousin had summoned him to her rescue; and, what was more galling to the young sheikh's pride, that she had been trifling with his affections, in order to gain the necessary time. He experienced a strong reaction of feeling from that mood of tenderness in which a few moments before he had been regretting the assembling of the sheikhs. In the presence of this new danger he saw it was his only chance; for, after all, she was a Druse maiden, she belonged to her people, and, if they decided upon her lot definitely, all the foreigners in the world were powerless to interfere with their decision, so long, at all events, as she remained a Turkish subject, and did not belong, as he had been careful to ascertain, to any sect of the Christian religion which might give a foreign power a right of interference on religious grounds. It was in no doubting or half-hearted mood, then, that he led the way across the *meidan* to the *manzil* in Sheikh Mohanna's yard, where he found the sheikh, who had been notified of the approach of the party, waiting to receive it, attended by his two friends.

It would have been impossible to imagine, from the air of dignified cordiality with which he received his guests, including Shibley, that Mohanna knew that one of them had lately attempted his life, and that their object in meeting now was to accuse him of being a traitor to his religion and his nation. That unruffled serenity and benign repose of manner indicated a sense of superiority over all those by whom he was surrounded, none the less marked because it sat so unconsciously upon its possessor, and irritated those of his guests who tried to imitate it, just in the degree that they were conscious in failing. When half an hour had elapsed, which was devoted to minute inquiries after the health of every individual sheikh, the Khateeb approached the business of the day by a long panegyric upon the learning, the virtues, the generosity, and the general reputation of Sheikh Mohanna; he further congratulated him upon the recovery of his niece, upon her estimable character, her charity, her intelligence, and other good qualities, and called to mind that this was not the first time he had alluded to them in connection with her religious views. He now explained that his duty as Khateeb required of him to ask Sheikh Mohanna whether he had fulfilled his promise of instructing his niece in such of the mysteries of their religion as were permitted to women to know; and whether she was prepared in the prescribed manner to give in her adhesion to it.

When this long harangue, which I have endeavoured to condense as much as possible, was terminated, Sheikh Mohanna bowed his head, and, in a tone in which there was a slight tinge of irony, replied—" My niece having had some reason to believe that the question which the Khateeb has so delicately and opportunely raised might come up for discussion to-day, begged me to express her desire to come before you herself and explain her own views in regard to it."

To this unexpected suggestion the Khateeb strongly objected; but the temptation of seeing Amina was too powerful for Shibley to resist, and he eagerly accepted the proposition. A warm discussion ensued in consequence, in which, as Sheikhs Mahmoud and Ibrahim supported Shibley, and carried many with them, the Khateeb was finally overborne, and it was decided that Amina should be invited to appear. The curiosity of many of the sheikhs to see her no doubt largely influenced this decision. Sheikh Mohanna insisted upon going himself to bring her, a proceeding which excited a good deal of unfavourable comment, as displaying a great lack of dignity on his part. In a few moments he returned, accompanied by Sada and Amina, both wearing veils, through which their features were indistinctly visible.

" The sheikhs here assembled," said Sheikh Mohanna, addressing his niece, who remained standing, " desire to be informed whether, now that you are instructed in all the mysteries of our religion which it is permitted to a woman to know, you are ready to adopt the faith of your people ? "

" It is impossible for me," answered Amina, " to adopt any religion in which women are excluded from knowledge which is permitted to men, as I do not believe that the Lord Hakeem intended any such distinction to be made—the divine feminine principle not being in fact inferior to the divine masculine, for inferiority is not possible to any divine attribute.

If the Druses recognise the equality of the
divine feminine, so they must recognise the
equality of the human feminine. My request
therefore is that I may be initiated into all the
knowledge permitted to man. .I believe that
the Okâls of my own nation are too intelligent
to expect me to adopt a religion, the knowledge
of which is in great part withheld from me."

This short speech, delivered not in the
pleasant dialect common to Druse women, but
in classical Arabic, and with perfect calm and
self-possession, so far from exciting the assembly by its audacity, as might have been
expected, seemed rather to stupefy it. It
raised a question which every man present
felt was entirely new to the whole nation.
To grant Amina's request was evidently impossible. It would alter the whole status of
Druse women. Even if an exception were to
be made in her favour, they were not an assembly powerful enough to grant such a privilege;
on the other hand, to coerce her to belong to a
religion which she only desired first to be
allowed to understand, seemed as she had put
it to be only reasonable, though no woman
had ever desired such knowledge before.

"Are you of opinion, O sheikh," said Sheikh Mahmoud, suddenly breaking the silence and addressing the Khateeb, "that the 'universal soul,' which represents the feminine principle, is inferior to the 'universal mind,' which represents the masculine?"

"Assuredly," said the Khateeb; and a discussion arose upon the point, which was felt to be a momentary relief. Meantime Shibley was getting impatient.

"We are assembled here to-day," he broke in at length, "to consider other questions besides the one raised by the Khateeb, in which both my cousin and I are deeply concerned. Is seems to me to be a matter of secondary importance whether she accords us her consent in her views upon religious matters. What is important is, that she should not repudiate her race as well as her religion, and deny the duties she owes to her own family. She has come back to us with treasure which would raise the villages peopled by her relatives to a position of affluence. It would not be acting according to Druse custom for her to carry all this away, and bestow it upon some Franji whom she may wish to wed. As a Druse maiden

—whether she chooses to say she is one in religion or not, does not matter—she is not permitted to wed a foreigner, much less to bestow her wealth upon him. As her nearest male relative, I claim both her hand and her money. I have the consent of her mother, as she will tell you, to our wedding; but Sheikh Mohanna refuses his. I maintain, as head of her family, that Sheikh Mohanna has no right or title to dispute my authority in this matter; and I appeal to you, O sheikhs, for your approval of the step I propose to take this day, which is to remove her, together with her property, from this house to my own, and there make her my wife."

This whole proposition was so simple, the idea of the girl going away and bestowing her wealth on a foreigner was so monstrous, and the fact that Shibley had privately promised a substantial *douceur* out of it to all who were now helping him to get it, was so potent an argument in favour of his cause, that with the exception of Mohanna and his two friends, who remained silent, a chorus of unanimous voices supported Shibley in the view he took of his own rights and duties; and

in their enthusiasm the sheikhs announced
that they would themselves escort her with
their retinues to Ain Ghazal that same afternoon.

"I shall not permit my niece to be carried
away against her will, until I have exhausted
every means of resistance, and, for reasons
which I will presently bring forward, I deny
the right which Sheikh Shibley arrogates to
himself to interfere in this matter." So saying,
Sheikh Mohanna made a sign to Sada, who
immediately left the room.

"It will be better for you not to increase
the animosity you have already excited against
yourself," said Shibley, flushed with the arro-
gance of a success which seemed certain, " by
appealing to a trial of strength with the
sheikhs now present. I had hoped to be
spared making the accusation against you, for
which the secret presence in your house for
more than two weeks past of a couple of un-
believers of bad character has given occasion,
and this for the purpose of screening the double
crime which they attempted to commit. Let
me have my way in peace, and I will trouble
you no more. Resist us, and we will not only

overbear any force you can bring against us now, and carry off my bride; but we will summon you to answer for opposing the decision of the council before those competent to judge of so weighty a matter, and at the same time bring against you these other charges by which we will prove your treachery to your race and your religion."

"Peace!" said Sheikh Mahmoud authoritatively; "this is not language which a youth of Sheikh Shibley's years should use to an elder whose long and useful life is in itself the best disproof of his rash assertions. Sheikh Mohanna has told us that he denies the right of Sheikh Shibley to interfere in this matter as the head of his cousin Amina's family, and has expressed his readiness to make good his position. Let us call upon him to do so. For it is evident that if he can succeed in this, there is no longer ground for dispute."

"This is mere folly," exclaimed Shibley angrily. "Will he dare to deny that I am the only son of my father, who was Sheikh Sâleh's nearest male relative?"

"No," said Sheikh Mohanna; "I will not

deny that; but I will prove that your birth
confers upon you none of the rights you claim.
Behold!" he added in a loud voice, pointing to
the door which Sada was now entering followed
by a tall Druse sheikh, "behold, Sheikh Shibley,
and sheikhs here assembled, the head of the
ancient family of Zedaan!"

An exclamation of astonishment burst from
the lips of several of the older sheikhs who had
known or remembered the late Sheikh Sâleh
in his early years, at a resemblance so marked
that it seemed as though Sheikh Mohanna had
conjured the old sheikh himself back to life
and youth. The whole group rose impulsively
to their feet, as Sheikh Mohanna stepped forward to receive and introduce the stranger.
He was a strikingly handsome man of seven
or eight and twenty, with regular features, a
clear dark complexion, a black moustache, but
otherwise closely shaved, and piercing black
eyes. He wore a snow - white turban, a
long robe of orange-coloured Damascus satin,
bound round the waist with a shawl-girdle,
over which was an *abayeh*, or cloak of fine
dark brown woollen reps, richly embroidered
with silk on the shoulders. His loose white

trousers were thrust into boots, reaching nearly to the knee, of red leather; his bearing was at once dignified and graceful.

"I am grateful for the opportunity with which Sheikh Shibley has furnished me," said Mohanna, leading the young man forward, "of presenting to so many illustrious sheikhs here assembled Sheikh Abdullah Zedaan, the only son of Sheikh Sâleh Zedaan, who was saved with his sister Amina, twenty-five years ago, at the time of the massacre, and like her carried off by the foreigners who were present at it, and who, believing all their family to have been murdered, brought them to Damascus. Amina was, as many of you will have by this time heard, adopted by Daoud Effendi Masollam, who is at this moment a guest in my house. The boy was cared for by the Englishman who was here with my friend Girius Bey on that fatal night. He and his wife took him with them to England, and she, dying childless soon after, made it her last request to her husband that the child they had brought from Syria, for whom she had conceived a warm affection, should be brought up by her husband as his own son.

But here come those who can furnish you with
fuller details and more ample proof than I
can do of the truth of this statement."

As he thus abruptly concluded, Santalba
and Masollam entered the room. Both Sheikh
Shibley and the Khateeb had been so utterly
taken aback by this most unlooked-for turn
of events, that they remained silent during a
general introduction which now took place
between the new arrivals and the sheikhs—
the latter being only too glad, by an excess
of civility towards Sheikh Mohanna and his
guests, to efface the unfavourable impression
which their recent attitude in support of
Shibley might have produced. They were
sufficiently shrewd to perceive that the cause
of the latter was lost, without waiting for
further proof of Sheikh Abdullah's identity,
and were quite disposed to pay court to the
rising sun of the house of Zedaan. They
struggled who should first kiss his hand and
do him honour, and in a few moments the
circle was again formed and seated, including
this time the three new-comers, while Sheikh
Mohanna insisted that Amina and her mother
should occupy places on the carpet by his side.

Then turning to Santalba, Sheikh Mohanna said—

"And now, O Girius Bey, will you narrate to the sheikhs here present the history of the rescue and subsequent life of Sheikh Abdullah."

To the surprise of the company, Santalba responded to this appeal in the purest Arabic.

"Know then, O sheikhs," he began, "that on that fatal night, the recollection of which is still fresh in your memories, I was a guest in this house with a dear friend of mine, an Englishman now dead, by name Hartwright. Being foreigners, we not only escaped the general massacre ourselves, but succeeded in snatching the two children, one a mere baby, and the boy, about two years old, from the knife of the assassins. Supposing that their parents and all their relations had been killed, we took them with us to Damascus, where my friend had left his wife. The girl we left with Daoud Effendi Masollam, the boy Mr and Mrs Hartwright took to England. Then Mrs Hartwright died, leaving him in charge of her husband, who had him educated and brought up as his own son, in complete ignorance of

his origin, which he never revealed to him up
to the day of his death. He was a man of
immense wealth, the whole of which he left in
my charge, to be given to his adopted son
when he arrived at the age at which, by English law, he would be entitled to hold it. At
the same time he made me his guardian, and
left it to my discretion to reveal his history to
him or not, as I might judge best. For some
years I did not feel that the time had come
when I should make this revelation. In the
meantime he entered the Parliament or governing council of his country, and owing to his
great wealth became a person of some consequence. Quite recently circumstances arose
which made it necessary, in my opinion, to
tell him that by birth he was a Druse; but I,
at the same time, extracted from him a promise that he would not disclose this fact to
any one without first consulting me. There
were many reasons why, in his own interests,
I thought this desirable, with which I need
not trouble you. The only other persons in
the secret were Daoud Effendi Masollam and
his wife. The former is here present to confirm the truth of my statements; and if any

further proof were wanting, there is the recognition of a birth-mark by his mother, who acknowledges him as her long-mourned son, and the striking resemblance which he bears to his father, and which must be apparent to all those among you who are old enough to remember Sheikh Sâleh."

Here there was a general chorus of assent on the part of all the older sheikhs, many of whom had repeatedly interrupted Girius Bey's narrative by exclamations of wonder and delight, more especially when they learned that the new sheikh was a man of wealth and influence, and actually a member of the governing council in England. The whole Druse nation was already assuming in their eyes a new and more important position in the world from that which it had hitherto occupied, and a suspicion began to arise in the minds of one or two of the more enthusiastic, that their newly discovered sheikh might be none other than the long-looked-for Druse Messiah in person.

As Sebastian became aware that all eyes were fixed upon him with wonder and admiration, he felt moved to speak.

" Will you explain to the sheikhs," he said,

using Santalba as his interpreter, "that there ·
are occasions when no language, even that
with which one is familiar, can express the
feelings which agitate the breast, and that it
must be therefore doubly painful to me not to
be able even to try and say what my heart is
full of, in my mother tongue, when my mother
is present, and so many near relatives? Tell
them—and I speak for my sister here as well
as for myself—that though we have been
brought up in strange lands, we can never
forget that we are Druses, and that whatever
knowledge or wealth or influence we possess,
we shall use only under a sense of the responsibility which we feel towards our own people,
and remembering the claims which they have
upon us; but they must see that we can be of
most service to them by retaining our independence, and using the position and influence
which our connection with another country
gives us for their advantage. In the meantime, however, I intend, by spending much of
my life in my native village, to acquire that
knowledge of my people, and of their customs
and language, as may enable me to identify
myself with their interests, and qualify me for

any duties which Providence may assign to me in relation to them."

When Santalba had finished interpreting this speech, Sheikh Mohanna turned to Shibley.

"I will not throw a cloud over this auspicious moment," he said, looking more especially at the young sheikh, but addressing all present, "by any further allusion to the subject which brought us hither, excepting to say that I have already banished it from my mind, and that I entertain no ill feeling towards any one who is now present. In evidence of which I beg you all to remain here as my guests to-night, and to share in the rejoicings which are to take place to-morrow, when many more sheikhs whom I have invited will arrive to celebrate, in a proper manner, the joyful return to his home and to his people of this worthy representative of the noble house of Zedaan— Sheikh Abdullah, whom may God long preserve!"

A murmur of applause followed this speech, amid which Mohanna rose, when Shibley, whose eyes had been constantly turned upon Amina, rushed forward impetuously and kissed the old sheikh's hand.

" God forgive you, my son," said the venerable man, in a tone of tenderness, " and may He train that fiery nature of yours to His service. Thank Him that He has given you relatives now, who will not only prompt you to high resolves, but will help you to keep them."

Shibley turned to Amina, cursing in his heart the etiquette of his people, which prevented him from even offering her his hand.

" Embrace my brother," she whispered with a smile.

And Shibley, in the presence of the assembly he had convoked to support him in his rights, obeyed her mandate, and by so doing, acknowledged that the Headship of the House of Zedaan belonged to Sheikh Abdullah.

CHAPTER XVI.

CONCLUSION.

THE festivities at Teraya had lasted for two days. From far and near had trooped Sheikhs and their retainers, eager to celebrate the return of the young chief. For the last twenty-four hours the firing of guns, the squealing of pipes, the drumming on tom-toms, the shrill scream of the women, the loud singing of the dancing choruses, both male and female, had been incessant. Now the last sheikh and his retinue had taken his departure, and a sudden stillness, all the more striking by its contrast with the recent discordant clamour, had supervened. The shades of the lovely autumnal evening were settling over the landscape when the party, which were so soon to leave Amina's wild home in the

mountains, were gathered on the terrace, to
enjoy the first moment of quiet which they
had been allowed since the startling disclosure
had been made which we have recounted in
the last chapter. Sebastian had adapted himself with marvellous facility to the new *rôle*
which he had been called upon so suddenly to
perform. Perhaps it came to him the more
easily as an hereditary instinct; but although
he was unable to speak a word of the language
of his people, the ease and dignity of his manner, and the art with which he acquired and
imitated all their forms of etiquette, combined
with his good looks and resemblance to his
father, made him popular; while the fact that
he was known to possess, what to them seemed
fabulous wealth, invested him with a prestige
which the mystery that had attended his
sudden appearance among them had been
eminently calculated to augment. In the
degree, however, in which he had shown
verve and skill in playing his part, had poor
Florence been bewildered and dismayed. From
her the secret had been religiously kept until
the day before the public disclosure, when
Santalba had revealed it to her in the presence

of her husband and Sheikh Mohanna. The idea that the cousin whom she had known as such from childhood was not her cousin Sebastian at all, but the Druse Sheikh Abdullah, was a fact so startling, that she only by degrees realised all that it implied, when she saw him, with his beard shaved off and in his national costume, struggling to kiss the hands of sheikhs, and receiving the homage of his inferiors. Then it seemed as if she had not only lost her cousin, but her husband, or else had fallen a victim to magic in some enchanted land.

"Don't you think I had better dress like a Druse woman, Sebastian, dear?" she had said. "I don't feel as if I was married to you at all while our clothes are so different."

And Amina had laughingly arrayed her for the time in Druse attire,—a compliment to the feminine population of the village which they much appreciated; while her husband declared that he had never before realised the full extent of her beauty. She was now gazing dreamily over the landscape, with her hand in Amina's, while her husband, Clareville, and Santalba, were lazily stretched near

them on cushions, exhausted apparently by
the fatigue and excitement of the last two
days.

"So it is settled, is it," she said, looking at
Sebastian, "that we are only to stay here two
days more?"

"I think that ought to be enough to rest
us thoroughly after all that we have gone
through, and the longer we delay our departure, the longer will our return be delayed.
Half the duties of our lives for the future lie
here; and I want to lose no time in making
arrangements which shall enable me to adapt
them to these new conditions. Besides, Amina
and Reginald have a little arrangement to
make which I do not think they wish to postpone, and which it is my duty to see consum-
mated. If I have lost a cousin, you must
remember that I have gained a sister, over
whom a council of sheikhs have solemnly declared I have all the rights of a guardian."

"But you neglected them," said Amina,
smiling, "long after you knew of our relationship."

"That was my fault," interrupted Saint-
alba; "and I am glad of the opportunity of

explaining much that must have seemed unaccountable to you all during our stay at The Turrets. When Masollam discovered Sada, and announced his intention of bringing her to England for the purpose of restoring her son to her, I received a shock which, while it produced an unpleasant impression, did not arouse my suspicion as to the purity of his motives. Sebastian's father had left it to my judgment, and not to that of Masollam, when the revelation of his origin should be made to him, if ever. When he did so, however, he believed that Sebastian's own mother was dead; and I felt that Masollam might fairly feel a responsibility in keeping a mother wilfully in ignorance of her son's existence. Moreover, I was accustomed to regard his intuitions in all matters of importance as derived from so high a source as to partake very much of the character of a command. At all events, he did not wait for my consent, but appeared with Tigranuhe and Amina one day in Paris, with the intelligence that Sada had already preceded him some months before to England with Carabet. Then, as you may remember, Amina, it was arranged that you

should go over to London and spend a few
days with the Cottrells, and, if possible, see
Sebastian and his great friend Reginald Clareville, whom I had felt from the first day I saw
him was destined sooner or later to be one of
us. You ask how I could have known this
on so slight an acquaintance," he continued,
turning to Reginald; "I can only answer, that
your nature was suddenly presented to my
inner consciousness as an image, revealing
what you really were in the depths of your
character, and not in that external presentation
of it by which you were yourself deceived, and
by which you deceived the world. Society
forces us to wear masks, to which we become
so accustomed, that we begin to regard them
as our own moral features, so to speak, when,
in fact, they are assumed to protect the most
precious and divine parts of us from the rough
contact of the civilisation in the midst of
which we are compelled to live. And this is
why, doubtless, Providence has provided us
with a retreat here, to which we can retire
when the outside pressure becomes insupport-
able, and in the intimacy of our own circle,
remove our masks and be ourselves, each a

protection to the other, and all encouraging the growth of those tender shoots which the process of a divine evolutionary growth is putting forth in us, sheltered from the blasts of the social tempest.

" Amina had not been more than three days in England when we received a telegram from Carabet, whom Masollam had settled in Tongsley to obtain information in regard to the Hartwright family, that the Charles Hartwrights were suddenly about to leave the country. I had already explained to Masollam the relations which existed between Sebastian and his cousin; and he felt that his whole project of winning Sebastian to our cause would be imperilled if he failed to avert a marriage which he saw to be imminent. I still had too much faith in the Master to imagine that he had any designs over Sebastian's fortune for his own private ends. I believed he was working from the same motive that I was, and with the same object in view, which, under God's providence, has been achieved, and which was to identify him with the effort of our lives, and enlist him in our cause. I gave him a letter of intro-

duction, therefore, to Charles Hartwright; but
he soon found himself unable alone to cope
with the difficulties of the situation, and, as
you remember, telegraphed for us. But even
had this summons not arrived, I should not
have delayed my departure for England, so
thoroughly had my suspicions been aroused
by Tigranuhe of her own honesty, not merely
of motive, but of act. Whether Masollam
was her accomplice or her dupe remained yet
to be discovered. I hoped the latter might
be the case, because I discovered that she was
carrying on a private correspondence with
Carabet unknown to the Master, and had
even gone so far as to tell her brother of
the existence of Sada's son. This knowledge
I turned to account on the occasion of our
first interview with Masollam after our arrival at The Turrets, and from that moment
Tigranuhe and I became uncompromising
foes. I soon found, however, to my deep
distress, that her influence had completely
sapped the moral character of him whom I
was accustomed to call the Master, the first
evidence of which was the reproach with
which he greeted me on finding that I had

been left heir to all Richard Hartwright's property by will, and had, in obedience to the verbal request of my friend on his death-bed, transferred it all intact to Sebastian on his coming of age. Masollam had heard of this for the first time from Charles Hartwright, and insisted that such a request was not binding in the presence of the far higher interests to which, if I had handed the money to him, he could have applied it."

"Why did Mr Hartwright leave the money to you, and not directly to Sebastian?" asked Amina.

"Because he would have been compelled to state in his will that Sebastian was not his son, and he did not wish to deprive him of the power of concealing his origin if he chose. The painful discovery of the utter extinction of all moral sense on the part of the Masollams, revealed to me a danger in the pursuit of truth, even for the highest motives, at which I was appalled, and by which, for the moment, I felt paralysed. It opened up the old problem which some of the Churches have settled to their satisfaction, and the solution of which in their sense has justified the horrors of the Inquisition, the foulest tyranny, the bloodiest wars, and the most relentless persecution. In conversation with Masollam, I found that he believed that he had reached a point of purity and excellence where he was the supreme judge of right and wrong. Because the world's standard was low, he had substituted one of his own manufacture, by which any means were justified by the loftiness of the aim in view. As murder ceases to be crime when it is committed in self-defence, so nothing could be criminal which was done in defence of the divine and humanitarian interests with which he believed himself to be intrusted : hence all that the world esteems wrong was sanctified by the moral pinnacle upon which he had perched himself, if it became expedient for the protection of the destinies of the human race, of which he believed himself the sole divine custodian ; or if rendered necessary by experiments made in the pursuit of truth. The fallacy of this reasoning lies in the fact that no one Church can dare to assert that it is the sole repository of divine truth, and, *a fortiori*, this is still more true of a man. Such an assumption opens the door to unbridled licence under the loftiest pretexts, until—unless the practice be checked—the world would be full of religious teachers, more corrupt than the society they professed to reform. In Masollam's case, I believe that he was more deceived than deceiving, and that he would not have fallen into the depths of treachery and dishonesty, from which he has now so providentially been rescued, had it not been for the insidious manner in which Tigranuhe pandered to his instincts of avarice, and fostered his spiritual pride. As it was, I found myself suddenly placed in a new and altogether unexpected position. It became necessary for me, without a day's delay, to endeavour to counteract the machinations which I had been myself innocently instrumental in assisting to contrive. Masollam's calculation had been, that the moral effect which would be produced upon Sebastian by the sudden revelation of his origin, and his introduction to his mother and sister, would so completely crush him, that, under our united influence, he would abandon England for ever, surrendering his purse for the great work which Masollam would propose to accomplish spiritually among the

Druse people, and come out here as his humble
disciple. But combinations more powerful
than any which Masollam, or the influences
behind him could form, were at work to
thwart these designs. Our friend Reginald
here had introduced a new set of complica-
tions," and Santalba glanced slily at Amina,
"upon which Masollam had not counted.
Through him, and her he loved, the foe
made a secret entrance into Masollam's citadel,
and roused within him passions which con-
trolled his judgment ; and the battle began,
which ended in that strategic movement to
the rear, which left Masollam master of the
field topographically, but spiritually routed at
all points. In the course of this battle, it became necessary for me to tell Sebastian of his
relationship to Sada ; but there were reasons
why the time had not come for either his
sister, or his mother, or his wife, to be en-
lightened upon a point, the premature knowledge of which would have disturbed their
mental balance at a time when each had as
much to bear as she could endure. That
is the reason, Amina, why Sebastian seemed
to have neglected his duty of guardian to

you, after he had become aware of his relationship; and, after all, you had Reginald."

"And," interposed Amina, with tears in
her eyes, placing her hand in Santalba's, "our
dearest friend, to whom we all owe everything."

"But who is only a weak instrument in
God's hands. Never did I feel so utterly
weak and impotent myself, as in those critical moments, when God was putting forth
His greatest power through me. Nor could
I have supposed it possible, knowing what
Masollam once was, that I should ever have
been able to free myself, much less to rescue
others from his magical influence. It seemed
a miracle at the time, but since then a greater
miracle has been performed in him and through
him."

"How so?" asked Reginald.

"He has done what I failed to do; he has
freed himself. Not altogether unassisted, it
is true; the passion which was once so fatal
to him, was used again to thwart the designs
of the woman to whom he was in bondage.
It impelled him to an act of violence which
broke the spell; and now she is chained and
bound, impotent for mischief, though un-

softened within. There is nothing changed
in her morally, but she is deprived of all
faculty of operation : she is like a caged wild
beast; her evil passions beat in vain against
the bars of her physical organism, but are
powerless to express themselves.   There is
no reason, so far as I can see, why she should
not linger in her present state for years;
and the one torture of her life, — but he
must never suspect it,—will be to be waited
upon by Masollam.   And this, he himself
knows, will be his only duty.   He is sane, and
in his right mind once more, but those wonderful gifts which he misused are taken from
him; his marvellous faculty is blighted.   He
will make a tender and thoughtful sick-nurse,
and find a melancholy pleasure in soothing
to the end the pillow of the poor creature to
whom he is bound for life, and he will live
a pure and blameless life, for there will be
no temptation to him to live otherwise.   He
is a charge given to us to cherish and protect,
for he has been a faithful and a valiant servant of his Master in his day, and we all owe
him much.   He was placed in the forefront
of the fight, and if he has been overcome in

the struggle, which of us can assert that in the same position we should have done better?"

As he spoke, Masollam, leaning on Sheikh Mohanna's arm, approached.

"I have been explaining to Daoud Effendi," said the sheikh, "the proposal which Amina and her brother have made, with regard to his taking up his home here with me permanently, and we have been examining the fall of the rock, with the view of seeing whether the terrace cannot be extended, so as to enable an addition to be made to the house for his accommodation. I find that it is quite practicable, and I have succeeded in overcoming Daoud Effendi's scruples in the matter. He consents to remain with us, with his wife, as our guests."

"I do more than consent," said Masollam, with a smile, "I obey. Whom should I obey, if not the man to whom I tried to do the greatest injury that one man can do to another, and to deprive of his personal liberty, and who offers me in return a home for life?"

"We none of us know what we owe to the other," said Sebastian; "the greatest services men render to each other are often those of

which at the time both are unconscious. I feel
that you have done more for me indirectly
than I can ever do for you directly. And now,"
he continued, turning to Sheikh Mohanna,
"what have you arranged with Shibley?"

"He too accepts your offer. We are to
make all the arrangements for the purchase
by you of the village of Ain Ghazal at his
own terms, and with the proceeds he, and all
those of the people who desire to accompany
him, will emigrate to the Jebel Druse. The
Khateeb and his family have expressed the
desire, if you will purchase their property, of
accompanying him."

"Certainly," said Sebastian; "and to-
morrow we will all ride over to Ain Ghazal
to fix upon the site of the new house, which
is to be the future haven of refuge, not only
for ourselves, but for those who, one with us
in aim and in endeavour, seek a shelter from
the storms of the world—not to rest in permanently with peace and comfort, but in which
they may refit and re-equip themselves pre-
paratory to issuing forth again to encounter
them."

"Thus it is," said Santalba, "that Providence

provides conditions appropriate to the service
which He calls us to perform; and that in the
degree in which men are capable of receiving
and putting forth a higher quality of divine
force, will the sphere of their operations be
enlarged, and opportunities furnished for ap-
plying it to the most divers sorts and conditions of men. Hitherto the religious instinct
of the world has found expression in creeds
and forms of dogmatism more or less appropriate to the local conditions by which the
religious teacher, who was its exponent, found
himself surrounded; or at all events, it
speedily adapted his teaching to those conditions. But the new and higher religious
instinct which is awakening in humanity finds
its expression not in creed or in dogma, but
in service for the neighbour, inspired by love
for him, which is the Divine love flowing
through the human instrument who has prepared himself to receive it; and this is irre-
spective of country, race, or social surround-
ings. Thus you, Amina, as the future Lady
Clareville, and your brother, as Sebastian
Hartwright, will have precisely the same
work to do in the centre of the world's

civilisation, that will claim you in the wilds of Syria as the heads of the Druse family of Zedaan, and in each case you will be so placed socially as to be able to exercise a very considerable influence in both the spheres of your operation; while it is certain that London and Paris stand as sorely in need of a new moral impulsion as Teraya or Ain Ghazal. There are social, theological, and scientific barriers which impede the flow of the new divine life into the human organism in the modern Babylons of the West, which have no existence in these more primitive regions; and it may be that once again, as of old, the scene of its first operation will be in this ancient land of Palestine, within the borders of which you are about to build your new home."

THE END.

PRINTED BY WILLIAM BLACKWOOD AND SONS.

www.ingramcontent.com/pod-product-compliance
Lightning Source LLC
Chambersburg PA
CBHW030730280326
41926CB00086B/1079